Baking

This edition published in 2010
LOVE FOOD is an imprint of Parragon Books Ltd

Parragon
Queen Street House
4 Queen Street
Bath BA1 1HE, UK

ISBN: 978-1-4454-2231-2

Printed in China

Created by Terry Jeavons & Company

Notes for the Reader
This book uses both metric and imperial measurements. Follow the same units of measurement throughout; do not mix metric and imperial. All spoon measurements are level: teaspoons are assumed to be 5 ml, and tablespoons are assumed to be 15 ml. Unless otherwise stated, milk is assumed to be full fat, eggs and individual vegetables are medium, and pepper is freshly ground black pepper.

The times given are an approximate guide only. Preparation times differ according to the techniques used by different people and the cooking times may also vary from those given. Optional ingredients, variations or serving suggestions have not been included in the calculations.

Recipes using raw or very lightly cooked eggs should be avoided by infants, the elderly, pregnant women, convalescents and anyone suffering from an illness. Pregnant and breastfeeding women are advised to avoid eating peanuts and peanut products. Sufferers from nut allergies should be aware that some of the ready-made ingredients used in the recipes in this book may contain nuts. Always check the packaging before use.

Baking

introduction

Baking is without any doubt the most rewarding of culinary experiences. To mix together the most unpromising-looking collection of ingredients, put them in an oven and have them emerge as a truly delicious creation is nothing short of a miracle!

No wonder, then, that there is something of a mystery to the whole process that is often daunting to an inexperienced cook. In reality, however, it's nowhere near as difficult as it might appear to bake a sumptuous large cake, a melt-in-the-mouth muffin, your favourite pie, a loaf of bread to serve fresh from the oven or an elegant savoury tart – and these are just a few examples of the wonderful baking recipes you will find in this book.

There are several items of kitchen equipment that are worth investing in if you are planning to make baking a regular event. A selection of baking tins is a must – baking sheets and tart tins, as well as round and square cake tins of various sizes, including one or two of the 'springform' type to facilitate the removal of large cakes, tortes and cheesecakes.

Apart from this, a couple of generously sized mixing bowls, some wooden spoons and perhaps a hand-held electric mixer will be enough to get you started. A more expensive item of equipment that will pay for itself in no time is a multipurpose food mixer. The different attachments will enable you to mix cake batters and pastry, whisk egg whites, whip cream and knead bread dough with speed and efficiency. In the past, of course, cooks had no such gadgets to help them out, and there is a certain satisfaction in doing all of the

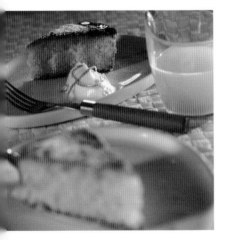

above tasks by hand – kneading bread dough for ten minutes is guaranteed to relieve tension, as well as produce a fabulous result.

Choose your favourite recipe, mix it with confidence and wait for the golden moment when you can bite into it!

cakes & gâteaux

Although a shop-bought cake is convenient and usually very good, a home-baked cake is so much better, perhaps because a little bit of the soul of the cook goes into it along with the other ingredients! If it doesn't come out looking absolutely perfect, it really doesn't matter – this just adds to its charm.

Different cakes suit different occasions, and you'll find a good cross-section here. For serving with morning coffee, try Gingerbread, Sticky Ginger Marmalade Loaf or Date & Walnut Loaf – these cakes improve with keeping, so can be wrapped in foil and stored in an airtight container for a few days. For an afternoon treat with tea, Sponge Cake, German Chocolate & Hazelnut Cake, Caribbean Coconut Cake, Honey Spiced Cake, Rich Fruit Cake and Banana & Lime Cake are perfect.

Some cakes make fabulous late-evening desserts – try a melting Torta de Cielo, fragrant Moroccan Orange & Almond Cake, moist Apple Streusel Cake or spicy Pear & Ginger Cake. Add a spoonful of whipped cream, ice cream, crème fraîche or thick yogurt, if you like.

And for those really special occasions? Chocolate Fudge Cake, Mocha Layer Cake, Coffee Caramel Cake, Chocolate Truffle Torte, Chocolate Cherry Layer Cake – you'll want to try them all!

chocolate fudge cake

ingredients

SERVES 8

175 g/6 oz unsalted butter,
   softened, plus extra
   for greasing
175 g/6 oz golden caster sugar
3 eggs, beaten
3 tbsp golden syrup
40 g/1½ oz ground almonds
175 g/6 oz self-raising flour
pinch of salt
40 g/1½ oz cocoa powder

icing

225 g/8 oz plain chocolate,
   broken into pieces
55 g/2 oz dark muscovado
   sugar
225 g/8 oz unsalted butter,
   diced
5 tbsp evaporated milk
½ tsp vanilla extract

method

1 Grease and line the bottom of 2 x 20-cm/ 8-inch round cake tins. To make the icing, place the chocolate, sugar, butter, evaporated milk and vanilla extract in a heavy-based pan. Heat gently, stirring constantly, until melted. Pour into a bowl and cool. Cover and chill in the refrigerator for 1 hour, or until spreadable.

2 Place the butter and sugar in a bowl and beat together until light and fluffy. Gradually beat in the eggs. Stir in the syrup and ground almonds. Sift the flour, salt and cocoa into a separate bowl, then fold into the mixture. Add a little water, if necessary, to make a dropping consistency. Spoon the mixture into the prepared tins and bake in a preheated oven, 180°C/350°F/Gas Mark 4, for 30–35 minutes, or until springy to the touch and a skewer inserted in the centre comes out clean.

3 Leave the cakes in the tins for 5 minutes, then turn out onto wire racks to cool completely. When the cakes are cold, sandwich them together with half the icing. Spread the remaining icing over the top and sides of the cake, swirling it to give a frosted appearance.

gingerbread

ingredients

MAKES 12–16 PIECES

450 g/1 lb plain flour
3 tsp baking powder
1 tsp baking soda
3 tsp ground ginger
175 g/6 oz butter
175 g/6 oz soft brown sugar
175 g/6 oz black molasses
175 g/6 oz golden syrup
1 egg, beaten
300 ml/10 fl oz milk

method

1 Line a 23-cm/9-inch square cake tin, 5 cm/2 inches deep, with baking paper.

2 Sift the flour, baking powder, baking soda and ginger into a large mixing bowl.

3 Place the butter, sugar, molasses and syrup in a medium pan and heat over low heat until the butter has melted and the sugar dissolved. Cool a little.

4 Mix the beaten egg with the milk and add to the cooled syrup mixture. Add the liquid ingredients to the flour mixture and beat well using a wooden spoon until the mixture is smooth and glossy.

5 Pour the mixture into the prepared tin and bake in the centre of a preheated oven, 160°C/325°F/Gas Mark 3, for $1^{1}/_{2}$ hours until well risen and just firm to the touch.

6 Remove from the oven and cool in the tin. When cool, remove the cake from the tin with the lining paper. Overwrap with foil and place in an airtight container for up to 1 week to allow the flavours to mature. Cut into wedges to serve.

sticky ginger marmalade loaf

ingredients

SERVES 10

175 g/6 oz butter, softened, plus extra for greasing

125 g/4½ oz ginger marmalade

175 g/6 oz brown sugar

3 eggs, beaten

225 g/8 oz self-raising flour

½ tsp baking powder

1 tsp ground ginger

100 g/3½ oz coarsely chopped pecans

method

1 Grease and line the bottom and ends of a 900-g/2-lb loaf tin. Place 1 tablespoon of the ginger marmalade in a small pan and reserve. Place the remaining marmalade in a bowl with the butter, sugar and eggs.

2 Sift in the flour, baking powder and ground ginger and beat together until smooth. Stir in three-quarters of the nuts. Spoon the mixture into the prepared loaf tin and smooth the top. Sprinkle with the remaining nuts and bake in a preheated oven, 180°C/350°F/Gas Mark 4, for 1 hour, or until well risen and a skewer inserted into the centre comes out clean.

3 Cool in the tin for 10 minutes, then turn out and peel off the lining paper. Transfer to a wire rack to cool until warm. Set the pan of reserved marmalade over low heat to warm, then brush over the loaf and serve in slices.

carrot cake

ingredients

MAKES 16 PIECES

2 eggs

175 g/6 oz molasses sugar

200 ml/7 fl oz sunflower oil

200 g/7 oz coarsely grated
  carrots

225 g/8 oz wholemeal flour

1 tsp baking soda

2 tsp ground cinnamon

whole nutmeg, grated
  (about 1 tsp)

115 g/4 oz roughly chopped
  walnuts

topping

115 g/4 oz half-fat
  cream cheese

4 tbsp butter, softened

85 g/3 oz icing sugar

1 tsp grated lemon rind

1 tsp grated orange rind

method

1 In a mixing bowl, beat the eggs until well blended and add the sugar and oil. Mix well. Add the grated carrot, sift in the flour, baking soda and spices, then add the walnuts. Mix everything together until well incorporated.

2 Grease and line a 20-cm/8-inch round cake tin. Spread the mixture into the prepared cake tin and bake in the centre of a preheated oven, 190°C/375°F/Gas Mark 5, for 40–50 minutes until the cake is nicely risen, firm to the touch and has begun to shrink away slightly from the edge of the tin. Remove from the oven and cool in the tin until just warm, then turn out onto a cooling rack.

3 To make the topping, put all the ingredients into a mixing bowl and beat together for 2–3 minutes until really smooth.

4 When the cake is completely cold, spread with the topping, smooth over with a fork, and allow to firm up a little before cutting into 16 portions. Store in an airtight container in a cool place for up to 1 week.

date & walnut loaf

ingredients

SERVES 10

175 g/6 oz butter, plus extra
    for greasing
225 g/8 oz pitted dates,
    chopped into small pieces
grated rind and juice
    of 1 orange
50 ml/2 fl oz water
175 g/6 oz brown sugar
3 eggs, beaten
85 g/3 oz wholemeal self-
    raising flour
85 g/3 oz self-raising flour
55 g/2 oz chopped walnuts
8 walnut halves
orange zest, to decorate

method

1 Grease and line the bottom and ends of a 900-g/2-lb loaf tin. Place the dates in a pan with the orange rind and juice and water and cook over medium heat for 5 minutes, stirring, or until a soft purée has formed.

2 Place the butter and sugar in a bowl and beat together until light and fluffy. Gradually beat in the eggs, then sift in the flours and fold in with the chopped walnuts. Spread one-third of the mixture over the bottom of the prepared loaf tin and spread half the date purée over the top.

3 Repeat the layers, ending with the cake mixture. Arrange walnut halves on top. Bake in a preheated oven, 160°C/325°F/Gas Mark 3, for 1–1¼ hours, or until well risen and firm to the touch. Cool in the tin for 10 minutes. Turn out, peel off the lining paper and transfer to a wire rack to cool. Decorate with orange zest and serve in slices.

sponge cake

ingredients

MAKES 8–10 SLICES

175 g/6 oz butter, at room
    temperature, plus extra
    for greasing
175 g/6 oz caster sugar
3 eggs, beaten
175 g/6 oz self-raising flour
pinch of salt

to serve

3 tbsp raspberry jam
1 tbsp caster or icing sugar

method

1 Grease 2 x 20-cm/8-inch round sponge cake tins and base-line with baking paper.

2 Beat the butter and sugar together in a mixing bowl using a wooden spoon or a hand-held mixer until the mixture is pale in colour and light and fluffy. Add the egg a little at a time, beating well after each addition.

3 Sift the flour and salt and carefully add to the mixture, folding it in with a metal spoon or a spatula. Divide the mixture between the tins and smooth over with the spatula. Place them on the same shelf in the centre of a preheated oven, 180°C/350°F/Gas Mark 4, and bake for 25–30 minutes until well risen, golden brown and beginning to shrink from the sides of the tins.

4 Remove from the oven and let stand for 1 minute. Loosen the cakes from around the edge of the tins using a round-bladed knife. Turn the cakes out onto a clean tea towel, remove the paper and invert them onto a wire rack (this prevents the wire rack from marking the top of the cakes). When completely cool, sandwich together with the jam and sprinkle with the sugar.

mocha layer cake

ingredients

SERVES 8

butter for greasing
200 g/7 oz self-raising flour
$1/4$ tsp baking powder
4 tbsp cocoa powder
100 g/$3^{1}/_{2}$ oz caster sugar
2 eggs
2 tbsp golden syrup
150 ml/5 fl oz corn oil
150 ml/5 fl oz milk

filling

1 tsp instant coffee
1 tbsp boiling water
300 ml/10 fl oz double cream
2 tbsp icing sugar

to decorate

50 g/$1^{3}/_{4}$ oz plain chocolate,
   grated
chocolate caraque
icing sugar, for dusting

method

1 Sift the flour, baking powder and cocoa into a large bowl, then stir in the sugar. Make a well in the centre and stir in the eggs, syrup, corn oil and milk. Beat with a wooden spoon, gradually mixing in the dry ingredients to make a smooth batter. Divide the mixture between 3 lightly greased 18-cm/7-inch cake tins.

2 Bake in a preheated oven, 180°C/350°F/Gas Mark 4, for 35–45 minutes, or until springy to the touch. Let stand in the tins for 5 minutes, then turn out and cool completely on a wire rack.

3 To make the filling, dissolve the instant coffee in the boiling water and place in a large bowl with the cream and icing sugar. Whip until the cream is just holding its shape, then use half the cream to sandwich the 3 cakes together. Spread the remaining cream over the top and sides of the cake. Press the grated chocolate into the cream round the edge of the cake.

4 Transfer the cake to a serving plate. Lay the chocolate caraque over the top of the cake. Cut a few thin strips of baking paper and place on top of the chocolate caraque. Dust lightly with icing sugar, then carefully remove the paper. Serve.

coffee caramel cake

ingredients

SERVES 8

175 g/6 oz butter, softened,
    plus extra for greasing
175 g/6 oz golden
    caster sugar
3 eggs, beaten
225 g/8 oz self-raising flour,
    sifted
100 ml/3^1/$_2$ fl oz strong
    black coffee
chocolate-covered coffee
    beans, to decorate

icing

125 ml/4 fl oz milk
125 g/4^1/$_2$ oz butter
3 tbsp golden caster sugar
575 g/1 lb 4^1/$_2$ oz icing sugar

method

1 Grease and base-line 2 x 20-cm/8-inch sponge cake tins. Place the butter and sugar in a bowl and beat together until light and fluffy. Gradually beat in the eggs, then fold in the flour and coffee. Divide the batter between the prepared tins and bake in a preheated oven, 180°C/350°F/Gas Mark 4, for 30 minutes, or until well risen and springy when pressed in the centre. Cool in the tins for 5 minutes, then turn out and peel off the lining paper. Transfer to wire racks to cool completely.

2 To make the icing, place the milk and butter in a pan, set over low heat and stir until the butter has melted. Remove the pan from the heat and set aside. Place the caster sugar in a separate, heavy-based pan and set over low heat, stirring constantly, until the sugar dissolves and turns a golden caramel. Remove from the heat and stir in the warm milk mixture. Return to the heat and stir until the caramel dissolves.

3 Remove from the heat and gradually stir in the icing sugar, beating until the icing is a smooth spreading consistency. Join the cakes together with some of the icing and spread the rest over the top and sides. Decorate with chocolate-covered coffee beans.

torta de cielo

ingredients

SERVES 4–6

225 g/8 oz unsalted butter,
   at room temperature, plus
   extra for greasing
175 g/6 oz whole almonds,
   in their skins
225 g/8 oz sugar
3 eggs, lightly beaten
1 tsp almond extract
1 tsp vanilla extract
9 tbsp plain flour
pinch of salt

to decorate

icing sugar, for dusting
slivered almonds, toasted

method

1 Lightly grease a 20-cm/8-inch round cake tin and line the tin with baking paper.

2 Place the almonds in a food processor and process to form a 'mealy' mixture. Set aside.

3 Beat the butter and sugar together in a large bowl until smooth and fluffy. Beat in the eggs, almonds and both the almond and vanilla extracts until well blended. Stir in the flour and salt and mix briefly, until the flour is just incorporated.

4 Pour or spoon the batter into the prepared tin and smooth the surface. Bake in a preheated oven, 180°C/350°F/Gas Mark 4, for 40–50 minutes, or until the cake feels spongy when gently pressed.

5 Remove from the oven and cool on a wire rack. To serve, dust with icing sugar and decorate with toasted slivered almonds.

chocolate truffle torte

ingredients

SERVES 10

butter, for greasing

55 g/2 oz golden caster sugar

2 eggs

25 g/1 oz plain flour

25 g/1 oz cocoa powder,
   plus extra to decorate

50 ml/2 fl oz cold strong
   black coffee

2 tbsp brandy

topping

600 ml/20 fl oz whipping
   cream

425 g/15 oz plain chocolate,
   melted and cooled

icing sugar, to decorate

method

1 Grease a 23-cm/9-inch springform cake tin with butter and line the bottom with baking paper. Place the sugar and eggs in a heatproof bowl and set over a pan of hot water. Whisk together until pale and mousse-like. Sift the flour and cocoa powder into a separate bowl, then fold gently into the cake batter. Pour into the prepared tin and bake in a preheated oven, 220°C/425°F/Gas Mark 7, for 7–10 minutes, or until risen and firm to the touch.

2 Transfer to a wire rack to cool. Wash and dry the tin and replace the cooled cake in the tin. Mix the coffee and brandy together and brush over the cake.

3 To make the topping, place the cream in a bowl and whip until very soft peaks form. Carefully fold in the cooled chocolate. Pour the chocolate mixture over the sponge and chill in the refrigerator for 4–5 hours, or until set.

4 To decorate the torte, sift cocoa powder over the top and remove carefully from the tin. Using strips of card or waxed paper as a mask, sift bands of icing sugar over the torte to create a striped pattern. To serve, cut into slices with a hot knife.

moroccan orange & almond cake

ingredients

SERVES 8

1 orange

115 g/4 oz butter, softened, plus extra for greasing

115 g/4 oz golden caster sugar

2 eggs, beaten

175 g/6 oz semolina

100 g/3^1/2 oz ground almonds

1^1/2 tsp baking powder

icing sugar, for dusting

strained plain yogurt, to serve

syrup

300 ml/10 fl oz orange juice

130 g/4^3/4 oz caster sugar

8 cardamom pods, crushed

method

1 Grate the rind from the orange, reserving some for the decoration, and squeeze the juice from one half. Place the butter, orange rind and sugar in a bowl and beat together until light and fluffy. Gradually beat in the eggs.

2 In a separate bowl, mix the semolina, ground almonds and baking powder, then fold into the creamed mixture with the orange juice. Spoon the batter into a greased and base-lined 20-cm/8-inch cake tin and bake in a preheated oven, 180°C/350°F/Gas Mark 4, for 30–40 minutes, or until well risen and a skewer inserted into the centre comes out clean. Cool in the tin for 10 minutes.

3 To make the syrup, place the orange juice, sugar and cardamom pods in a pan over low heat and stir until the sugar has dissolved. Bring to a boil and simmer for 4 minutes, or until syrupy.

4 Turn the cake out into a deep serving dish. Using a skewer, make holes over the surface of the warm cake. Strain the syrup into a separate bowl and spoon three-quarters of it over the cake, then set aside for 30 minutes. Dust the cake with icing sugar and cut into slices. Serve with the remaining syrup drizzled around, accompanied by strained plain yogurt decorated with the reserved orange rind.

german chocolate & hazelnut cake

ingredients

SERVES 8

175 g/6 oz unsalted butter,
    softened, plus extra
    for greasing
115 g/4 oz dark brown sugar
175 g/6 oz self-raising flour,
    plus extra for dusting
1 tbsp cocoa powder
1 tsp allspice
3 eggs, beaten
115 g/4 oz ground hazelnuts
2 tbsp black coffee
icing sugar, for dusting

method

1 Grease and flour a 19-cm/7^1/2-inch kugelhopf tin. Place the butter and brown sugar in a large mixing bowl and beat together until light and fluffy. Sift the self-raising flour, cocoa powder and allspice into a separate bowl.

2 Beat the eggs into the creamed batter, one at a time, adding 1 tablespoon of the flour mixture with the second and third eggs. Fold in the remaining flour mixture, ground hazelnuts and coffee.

3 Turn into the prepared tin and bake in a preheated oven, 180°C/350°F/Gas Mark 4, for 45–50 minutes, or until the cake springs back when lightly pressed. Cool in the tin for 10 minutes, then turn out onto a wire rack to cool completely. Dust generously with icing sugar before serving.

caribbean coconut cake

ingredients

SERVES 8

280 g/10 oz butter, softened,
   plus extra for greasing
175 g/6 oz golden caster
   sugar
3 eggs
175 g/6 oz self-raising flour
1½ tsp baking powder
½ tsp freshly grated nutmeg
55 g/2 oz dry unsweetened
   coconut
5 tbsp coconut cream
280 g/10 oz icing sugar
5 tbsp pineapple jam
dry unsweetened coconut,
   toasted, to decorate

method

1 Grease and base-line 2 x 20-cm/8-inch sponge cake tins. Place 175 g/6 oz of the butter in a bowl with the sugar and eggs and sift in the flour, baking powder and nutmeg. Beat together until smooth, then stir in the coconut and 2 tablespoons of the coconut cream into the mixture.

2 Divide the mixture between the prepared tins and smooth the surface. Bake in a preheated oven, 180°C/350°F/Gas Mark 4, for 25 minutes, or until golden and firm to the touch. Cool in the tins for 5 minutes, then turn out onto a wire rack, peel off the lining paper and cool completely.

3 Sift the icing sugar into a bowl and add the remaining butter and coconut cream. Beat together until smooth. Spread the pineapple jam on one of the cakes and top with just under half of the buttercream. Place the other cake on top. Spread the remaining buttercream on top of the cake and scatter with the toasted coconut.

honey spiced cake

ingredients

SERVES 8

150 g/5^1/$_2$ oz butter, plus
    extra for greasing
115 g/4 oz brown sugar
175 g/6 oz honey
1 tbsp water
200 g/7 oz self-raising flour
^{1}/$_2$ tsp ground ginger
^{1}/$_2$ tsp ground cinnamon
^{1}/$_2$ tsp caraway seeds
seeds from 8 cardamom pods,
    ground
2 eggs, beaten
350 g/12 oz icing sugar

method

1 Grease an 1-litre/1^3/$_4$-pint fluted cake tin. Place the butter, sugar, honey and water into a heavy-based pan. Set over low heat and stir until the butter has melted and the sugar has dissolved. Remove from the heat and cool for 10 minutes.

2 Sift the flour into a bowl and mix in the ginger, cinnamon, caraway seeds and cardamom. Make a well in the centre. Pour in the honey mixture and the eggs and beat well until smooth. Pour the batter into the prepared tin and bake in a preheated oven, 180°C/350°F/Gas Mark 4, for 40–50 minutes, or until well risen and a skewer inserted into the centre comes out clean. Cool in the tin for 5 minutes, then transfer to a wire rack to cool completely.

3 Sift the icing sugar into a bowl. Stir in enough warm water to make a smooth, flowing icing. Spoon over the cake, allowing it to flow down the sides, then allow to set.

rich fruit cake

ingredients

SERVES 4

butter, for greasing

175 g/6 oz pitted unsweetened
   dates

125 g/4^1/$_2$ oz no-soak dried
   prunes

200 ml/7 fl oz unsweetened
   orange juice

2 tbsp molasses

1 tsp finely grated lemon rind

1 tsp finely grated orange rind

225 g/8 oz wholemeal self-
   raising flour

1 tsp mixed spice

125 g/4^1/$_2$ oz seedless raisins

125 g/4^1/$_2$ oz sultanas

125 g/4^1/$_2$ oz currants

125 g/4^1/$_2$ oz dried cranberries

3 large eggs, separated

1 tbsp apricot jam, warmed

icing

125 g/4^1/$_2$ oz icing sugar

1–2 tsp water

1 tsp vanilla extract

orange and lemon rind strips,
   to decorate

method

1 Grease and line a deep 20-cm/8-inch round cake tin. Chop the dates and prunes and place in a pan. Pour over the orange juice and simmer for 10 minutes. Remove the pan from the heat and beat the fruit mixture until puréed. Add the molasses and citrus rinds and cool.

2 Sift the flour and spice into a bowl, adding any bran that remains in the sieve. Add the dried fruits. When the date and prune mixture is cool, whisk in the egg yolks. Whisk the egg whites in a separate, clean bowl until stiff. Spoon the fruit mixture into the dry ingredients and mix together.

3 Gently fold in the egg whites. Transfer to the prepared tin and bake in a preheated oven, 160°C/325°F/Gas Mark 3, for 1^1/$_2$ hours. Cool in the tin.

4 Remove the cake from the tin and brush the top with jam. To make the icing, sift the sugar into a bowl and mix with enough water and the vanilla extract to form a soft icing. Lay the icing over the top of the cake and trim the edges. Decorate with orange and lemon rind.

chocolate cherry layer cake

ingredients

SERVES 8

3 tbsp unsalted butter, melted,
plus extra for greasing
900 g/2 lb fresh cherries,
pitted and halved
250 g/9 oz caster sugar
100 ml/3^1/$_2$ fl oz cherry
brandy
100 g/3^1/$_2$ oz plain flour
50 g/1^3/$_4$ oz cocoa powder
^{1}/$_2$ tsp baking powder
4 eggs
1 litre/1^3/$_4$ pints double cream
grated plain chocolate
whole fresh cherries,
to decorate

method

1 Grease and line a 23-cm/9-inch springform cake tin. Put the halved cherries into a pan and add 3 tablespoons of the sugar and the cherry brandy. Simmer for 5 minutes. Strain, reserving the syrup. In another bowl, sift together the flour, cocoa and baking powder.

2 Put the eggs in a heatproof bowl and beat in 160 g/5^3/$_4$ oz of the sugar. Place the bowl over a pan of simmering water and beat for 6 minutes until thickened. Remove from the heat, then gradually fold in the flour mixture and melted butter. Spoon into the cake tin. Bake in a preheated oven, 180°C/350°F/Gas Mark 4, for 40 minutes. Remove from the oven and cool.

3 Turn out the cake and cut in half horizontally. Whip the cream with the remaining sugar. Spread the reserved syrup over the cut sides of the cake. Arrange the cherries over one half, top with a layer of cream and place the other half on top. Cover with cream, press grated chocolate all over and decorate with cherries.

blueberry & lemon drizzle cake

ingredients

SERVES 12

225 g/8 oz butter, softened,
 plus extra for greasing
225 g/8 oz golden caster
 sugar
4 eggs, beaten
250 g/9 oz self-raising flour,
 sifted
finely grated rind and juice
 of 1 lemon
25 g/1 oz ground almonds
200 g/7 oz fresh blueberries

topping

juice of 2 lemons
115 g/4 oz golden caster
 sugar

method

1 Grease and line the bottom of a 20-cm/ 8-inch square cake tin. Place the butter and sugar in a bowl and beat together until light and fluffy. Gradually beat in the eggs, adding a little flour toward the end to prevent curdling. Beat in the lemon rind, then fold in the remaining flour and almonds with enough of the lemon juice to give a good dropping consistency.

2 Fold in three-quarters of the blueberries and turn into the prepared tin. Smooth the surface, then scatter the remaining blueberries on top. Bake in a preheated oven, 180°C/350°F/ Gas Mark 4, for 1 hour, or until firm to the touch and a skewer inserted into the centre comes out clean.

3 To make the topping, place the lemon juice and sugar in a bowl and mix together. As soon as the cake comes out of the oven, prick it all over with a fine skewer and pour over the lemon mixture. Cool in the tin until completely cold, then cut into 12 squares to serve.

apple streusel cake

ingredients

SERVES 8

115 g/4 oz butter, plus extra
   for greasing
450 g/1 lb tart cooking apples
175 g/6 oz self-raising flour
1 tsp ground cinnamon
pinch of salt
115 g/4 oz golden caster
   sugar
2 eggs
1–2 tbsp milk
icing sugar, for dusting

streusel topping

115 g/4 oz self-raising flour
6 tbsp butter
85 g/3 oz golden caster sugar

method

1 Grease a 23-cm/9-inch springform cake tin. To make the streusel topping, sift the flour into a bowl and rub in the butter until the mixture resembles coarse crumbs. Stir in the sugar and set aside.

2 Peel, core and thinly slice the apples. To make the cake, sift the flour into a bowl with the cinnamon and salt. Place the butter and sugar in a separate bowl and beat together until light and fluffy. Gradually beat in the eggs, adding a little of the flour mixture with the last addition of egg. Gently fold in half the remaining flour mixture, then fold in the rest with the milk.

3 Spoon the batter into the prepared tin and smooth the top. Cover with the sliced apples and sprinkle the streusel topping evenly over the top. Bake in a preheated oven, 180°C/ 350°F/Gas Mark 4, for 1 hour, or until browned and firm to the touch. Cool in the tin before opening the sides. Dust the cake with icing sugar before serving.

banana & lime cake

ingredients

SERVES 10

butter, for greasing

300 g/10¹/₂ oz plain flour

1 tsp salt

1¹/₂ tsp baking powder

175 g/6 oz brown sugar

1 tsp grated lime rind

1 egg, beaten

1 banana, mashed with
   1 tbsp lime juice

150 ml/5 fl oz low-fat cream
   cheese

115 g/4 oz sultanas

topping

115 g/4 oz icing sugar

1–2 tsp lime juice

¹/₂ tsp finely grated lime rind

to decorate

banana chips

finely grated lime rind

method

1 Grease and line a deep 18-cm/7-inch round cake tin with baking paper. Sift the flour, salt and baking powder into a large bowl and stir in the sugar and lime rind.

2 Make a well in the centre of the dry ingredients and add the egg, banana, cream cheese and sultanas. Mix well until thoroughly incorporated. Spoon the batter into the tin and smooth the surface.

3 Bake in a preheated oven, 180°C/350°F/Gas Mark 4, for 40–45 minutes, until firm to the touch or until a skewer inserted in the centre comes out clean. Cool the cake in the tin for 10 minutes, then turn out onto a wire rack to cool completely.

4 To make the topping, sift the icing sugar into a small bowl and mix with the lime juice to form a soft, but not too runny icing. Stir in the grated lime rind. Drizzle the icing over the cake, letting it run down the sides. Decorate the cake with banana chips and lime rind. Allow the cake to stand for 15 minutes so that the icing sets.

pear & ginger cake

ingredients

SERVES 6

200 g/7 oz unsalted butter,
   softened, plus extra
   for greasing
175 g/6 oz caster sugar
175 g/6 oz self-raising flour,
   sifted
1 tbsp ground ginger
3 eggs, beaten lightly
450 g/1 lb pears, peeled, cored
   and thinly sliced, then
   brushed with lemon juice
1 tbsp brown sugar
ice cream or double cream,
   lightly whipped, to serve
   (optional)

method

1 Lightly grease a deep 20-cm/8-inch cake tin with butter and line the bottom with baking parchment.

2 Mix all but 2 tablespoons of the butter with the caster sugar, flour, ginger and eggs in a bowl. Beat with a whisk until the mixture forms a smooth consistency.

3 Spoon the cake batter into the prepared tin and level out the surface with a spatula. Arrange the pear slices over the cake batter. Sprinkle with the brown sugar and dot with the remaining butter.

4 Bake in a preheated oven, 180°C/350°F/ Gas Mark 4, for 35–40 minutes, or until the cake is golden on top and feels springy to the touch. Serve warm, with ice cream or whipped cream, if you like.

small
bites

Small bites – muffins, cupcakes, biscuits and slices – have a very special appeal, perhaps because they have a delightfully self-indulgent, 'just for me' feel about them!

Children love small bites, so they'll be thrilled to find a treat in their school lunchbox – a Drizzled Honey Cupcake, Apple & Cinnamon Muffin, Spiced Chocolate Muffin, Fruit & Nut Square or an Oat & Hazelnut Bite or two will revive them after the morning's exertions and set them up for the afternoon. When they get home from school, let them get their fingers sticky with a Iced Peanut Butter Cupcake, Sticky Gingerbread Cupcake, Banana & Pecan Cupcake or a Lemon Butterfly Cake – gorgeously messy!

Grown-ups – probably as an antidote to being grown up – love anything with a hint of wickedness and preferably more than a hint of chocolate! Devil's Food Cakes with Chocolate Icing, Chocolate Temptations and Warm Molten-centred Chocolate Cupcakes are satisfyingly naughty.

For more sedate adult occasions, Fudge Nut Muffins, Fig & Almond Muffins, Lavender Biscuits and Fig & Walnut Cookies are simply delicious, and a Rose Petal Cupcake, with its delicate pink icing, is a thoughtful treat to serve on a birthday or anniversary.

drizzled honey cupcakes

ingredients

MAKES 12

85 g/3 oz self-raising flour
$1/4$ tsp ground cinnamon
pinch of ground cloves
pinch of grated nutmeg
6 tbsp butter, softened
85 g/3 oz caster sugar
1 tbsp honey
finely grated rind of 1 orange
2 eggs, lightly beaten
40 g/1$1/2$ oz walnut pieces,
　chopped

topping

15 g/$1/2$ oz walnut pieces,
　chopped
$1/4$ tsp ground cinnamon
2 tbsp honey
juice of 1 orange

method

1 Put 12 paper baking cases in a muffin tin, or place 12 double-layer paper cases on a baking sheet.

2 Sift the flour, cinnamon, cloves and nutmeg together into a bowl. Put the butter and sugar in a separate bowl and beat together until light and fluffy. Beat in the honey and orange rind, then gradually add the eggs, beating well after each addition. Using a metal spoon, fold in the flour mixture. Stir in the walnuts, then spoon the batter into the paper cases.

3 Bake the cupcakes in a preheated oven, 190°C/375°F/Gas Mark 5, for 20 minutes, or until well risen and golden brown. Transfer to a wire rack to cool.

4 To make the topping, mix together the walnuts and cinnamon. Put the honey and orange juice in a pan and heat gently, stirring, until combined.

5 When the cupcakes have almost cooled, prick the tops all over with a fork or skewer and then drizzle with the warm honey mixture. Sprinkle the walnut mixture over the top of each cupcake and serve warm or cold.

iced peanut butter cupcakes

ingredients

MAKES 16

4 tbsp butter, softened,
    or soft margarine
225 g/8 oz brown sugar
115 g/4 oz crunchy
    peanut butter
2 eggs, lightly beaten
1 tsp vanilla extract
225 g/8 oz plain flour
2 tsp baking powder
100 ml/3$^1/_2$ fl oz milk

icing

200 g/7 oz full-fat soft cream
    cheese
2 tbsp butter, softened
225 g/8 oz icing sugar

method

1 Put 16 muffin paper cases in a muffin tin.

2 Put the butter, sugar and peanut butter in a bowl and beat together for 1–2 minutes, or until well mixed. Gradually add the eggs, beating well after each addition, then add the vanilla extract. Sift in the flour and baking powder and then, using a metal spoon, fold them into the mixture, alternating with the milk. Spoon the batter into the paper cases.

3 Bake the cupcakes in a preheated oven, 180°C/350°F/Gas Mark 4, for 25 minutes, or until well risen and golden brown. Transfer to a wire rack to cool.

4 To make the icing, put the cream cheese and butter in a large bowl and, using an electric hand whisk, beat together until smooth. Sift the icing sugar into the mixture, then beat together until well mixed.

5 When the cupcakes are cold, spread the icing on top of each cupcake, swirling it with a round-bladed knife. Store the cupcakes in the refrigerator until ready to serve.

rose petal cupcakes

ingredients

MAKES 12

8 tbsp butter, softened

115 g/4 oz caster sugar

2 eggs, lightly beaten

1 tbsp milk

few drops of extract of rose oil

1/4 tsp vanilla extract

175 g/6 oz self-raising flour

icing

6 tbsp butter, softened

175 g/6 oz icing sugar

pink or purple food colouring
   (optional)

silver dragées (cake decoration
   balls), to decorate

candied rose petals

12–24 rose petals

lightly beaten egg white,
   for brushing

caster sugar, for sprinkling

method

1 To make the candied rose petals, gently rinse the petals and dry well with kitchen paper. Using a pastry brush, paint both sides of a rose petal with egg white, then coat well with caster sugar. Place on a tray and repeat with the remaining petals. Cover the tray with foil and set aside to dry overnight.

2 Put 12 paper baking cases in a muffin tin, or place 12 double-layer paper cases on a baking sheet.

3 Put the butter and sugar in a bowl and beat together until light and fluffy. Gradually add the eggs, beating well after each addition. Stir in the milk, rose oil extract and vanilla extract then, using a metal spoon, fold in the flour. Spoon the batter into the paper cases.

4 Bake the cupcakes in a preheated oven, 200°C/400°F/Gas Mark 6, for 12–15 minutes until well risen and golden brown. Transfer to a wire rack to cool.

5 To make the icing, put the butter in a large bowl and beat until fluffy. Sift in the icing sugar and mix well together. If wished, add a few drops of pink or purple food colouring to complement the rose petals.

6 When the cupcakes are cold, spread the icing on top of each cake. Top with 1–2 candied rose petals and sprinkle with silver dragées to decorate.

sticky gingerbread cupcakes

ingredients

MAKES 16

115 g/4 oz plain flour
2 tsp ground ginger
$^3/_4$ tsp ground cinnamon
1 piece of preserved ginger, finely chopped
$^3/_4$ tsp baking soda
4 tbsp milk
6 tbsp butter, softened, or soft margarine
70 g/2$^1/_2$ oz brown sugar
2 tbsp molasses
2 eggs, lightly beaten
pieces of preserved ginger, to decorate

icing

6 tbsp butter, softened
175 g/6 oz icing sugar
2 tbsp ginger syrup from the preserved ginger jar

method

1 Put 16 paper baking cases in a muffin tin, or place 16 double-layer paper cases on a baking sheet.

2 Sift the flour, ground ginger and cinnamon together into a bowl. Add the chopped ginger and toss in the flour mixture until well coated. In a separate bowl, dissolve the baking soda in the milk.

3 Put the butter and sugar in a bowl and beat together until fluffy. Beat in the molasses, then gradually add the eggs, beating well after each addition. Beat in the flour mixture, then gradually beat in the milk. Spoon the batter into the paper cases.

4 Bake the cupcakes in a preheated oven, 160°C/325°F/Gas Mark 3, for 20 minutes, or until well risen and golden brown. Transfer to a wire rack to cool.

5 To make the icing, put the butter in a bowl and beat until fluffy. Sift in the sugar, add the ginger syrup and beat together until smooth and creamy. Slice the preserved ginger into thin slivers or chop finely.

6 When the cupcakes are cold, spread the icing on top of each cupcake, then decorate with pieces of ginger.

fudge nut muffins

ingredients

MAKES 12

250 g/9 oz plain flour

4 tsp baking powder

85 g/3 oz caster sugar

6 tbsp crunchy peanut butter

1 large egg, beaten

4 tbsp butter, melted

175 ml/6 fl oz milk

150 g/5^1/$_2$ oz vanilla fudge,
    cut into small pieces

3 tbsp coarsely chopped
    unsalted peanuts

method

1 Line a 12-cup muffin tin with double muffin paper liners. Sift the flour and baking powder into a bowl. Stir in the caster sugar. Add the peanut butter and stir until the mixture resembles breadcrumbs.

2 Place the egg, butter and milk in a separate bowl and beat until blended, then stir into the dry ingredients until just blended. Lightly stir in the fudge pieces. Divide the batter evenly between the muffin liners.

3 Sprinkle the chopped peanuts on top and bake in a preheated oven, 200°C/400°F/Gas Mark 6, for 20–25 minutes until well risen and firm to the touch. Remove the muffins from the oven and cool for 2 minutes, then place them on a wire rack to cool completely.

fig & almond muffins

ingredients

2 tbsp sunflower or peanut
   oil, plus extra for oiling
   (if using)
250 g/9 oz plain flour
1 tsp baking soda
$^1/_2$ tsp salt
225 g/8 oz raw sugar
85 g/3 oz dried figs, chopped
115 g/4 oz almonds, chopped
200 ml/7 fl oz water
1 tsp almond extract
2 tbsp chopped almonds,
   to decorate

method

1 Oil a 12-cup muffin tin with sunflower oil, or line it with 12 muffin paper liners. Sift the flour, baking soda and salt into a mixing bowl, then add the raw sugar and stir together.

2 In a separate bowl, mix the figs, almonds and remaining sunflower oil together, then stir in the water and almond extract. Add the fruit and nut mixture to the flour mixture and gently stir together. Do not overstir – it is fine for it to be a little lumpy.

3 Divide the muffin batter evenly between the 12 cups in the muffin tin or the paper liners (they should be about two-thirds full), then sprinkle over the remaining chopped almonds to decorate. Transfer to a preheated oven, 190°C/375°F/Gas Mark 5 and bake for 25 minutes, or until risen and golden.

4 Remove the muffins from the oven and serve warm, or place them on a wire rack to cool.

banana & pecan cupcakes

ingredients

MAKES 12

225 g/8 oz plain flour

$1^{1}/4$ tsp baking powder

$^{1}/4$ tsp baking soda

2 ripe bananas

8 tbsp butter, softened,
   or soft margarine

115 g/4 oz caster sugar

$^{1}/2$ tsp vanilla extract

2 eggs, lightly beaten

4 tbsp soured cream

55 g/2 oz pecans, coarsely
   chopped

topping

8 tbsp butter, softened

115 g/4 oz icing sugar

25 g/1 oz pecans, chopped

method

1 Line a 12-cup muffin tin with a double layer of muffin paper liners, or place 12 double-layer paper cases on a baking sheet.

2 Sift together the flour, baking powder and baking soda. Peel the bananas, put them in a bowl and mash with a fork.

3 Put the butter, sugar and vanilla in a bowl and beat together until light and fluffy. Gradually add the eggs, beating well after each addition. Stir in the mashed bananas and soured cream. Using a metal spoon, fold in the sifted flour mixture and the chopped nuts, then spoon the batter into the paper cases.

4 Bake the cupcakes in a preheated oven, 190°C/375°F/Gas Mark 5, for 20 minutes, or until well risen and golden brown. Transfer to a wire rack to cool.

5 To make the topping, beat the butter in a bowl until fluffy. Sift in the icing sugar and mix together well. Spread the icing on top of each cupcake and sprinkle with the chopped pecans before serving.

apple & cinnamon muffins

ingredients

MAKES 6

85 g/3 oz plain
   wholemeal flour
70 g/2^1/$_2$ oz plain flour
1^1/$_2$ tsp baking powder
pinch of salt
1 tsp ground cinnamon
40 g/1^1/$_2$ oz golden caster
   sugar
2 small eating apples, peeled,
   cored and finely chopped
125 ml/4 fl oz milk
1 egg, beaten
4 tbsp butter, melted

topping

12 brown sugar lumps,
   coarsely crushed
^{1}/$_2$ tsp ground cinnamon

method

1 Place 6 muffin paper liners in a muffin tin.

2 Sift both flours, baking powder, salt and cinnamon together into a large bowl and stir in the sugar and chopped apples. Place the milk, egg and butter in a separate bowl and mix. Add the wet ingredients to the dry ingredients and gently stir until just combined.

3 Divide the batter evenly between the paper liners. To make the topping, mix the crushed sugar lumps and cinnamon together and sprinkle over the muffins. Bake in a preheated oven, 200°C/400°F/ Gas Mark 6, for 20–25 minutes, or until risen and golden. Remove the muffins from the oven and serve warm or place them on a wire rack to cool.

moist walnut cupcakes

ingredients

MAKES 12

85 g/3 oz walnuts
4 tbsp butter, softened
100 g/3$^1/_2$ oz caster sugar
grated rind of $^1/_2$ lemon
70 g/2$^1/_2$ oz self-raising flour
2 eggs
12 walnut halves, to decorate

icing

4 tbsp butter, softened
85 g/3 oz icing sugar
grated rind of $^1/_2$ lemon
1 tsp lemon juice

method

1 Put 12 paper baking cases in a muffin tin, or place 12 double-layer paper cases on a baking sheet.

2 Put the walnuts in a food processor and, using a pulsating action, blend until finely ground, being careful not to overgrind, which will turn them to oil. Add the butter, cut into small pieces, along with the sugar, lemon rind, flour and eggs, then blend until evenly mixed. Spoon the batter into the paper cases.

3 Bake the cupcakes in a preheated oven, 190°C/375°F/Gas Mark 5, for 20 minutes, or until well risen and golden brown. Transfer to a wire rack to cool.

4 To make the icing, put the butter in a bowl and beat until fluffy. Sift in the icing sugar, add the lemon rind and juice and mix well.

5 When the cupcakes are cold, spread the icing on top of each cupcake and top with a walnut to decorate.

lemon butterfly cakes

ingredients

MAKES 12 CUPCAKES

115 g/4 oz self-raising flour
$1/2$ tsp baking powder
8 tbsp soft margarine
115 g/4 oz caster sugar
2 eggs, lightly beaten
finely grated rind of $1/2$ lemon
2 tbsp milk
icing sugar, for dusting

lemon filling

6 tbsp butter, softened
175 g/6 oz icing sugar
1 tbsp lemon juice

method

1 Put 12 paper baking cases in a muffin tin, or place 12 double-layer paper cases on a baking sheet.

2 Sift the flour and baking powder into a large bowl. Add the margarine, sugar, eggs, lemon rind and milk and, using an electric hand whisk, beat together until smooth. Spoon the batter into the paper cases.

3 Bake the cupcakes in a preheated oven, 190°C/375°F/Gas Mark 5, for 15–20 minutes, or until well risen and golden brown. Transfer to a wire rack to cool.

4 To make the filling, put the butter in a bowl and beat until fluffy. Sift in the icing sugar, add the lemon juice and beat together until smooth and creamy.

5 When the cupcakes are cold, use a serrated knife to cut a circle from the top of each cupcake and then cut each circle in half. Spread or pipe a little of the buttercream filling into the centre of each cupcake, then press the 2 semicircular halves into it at an angle to resemble butterfly wings. Dust the cakes with sifted icing sugar before serving.

warm molten-centred chocolate cupcakes

ingredients

MAKES 8

4 tbsp soft margarine
55 g/2 oz caster sugar
1 large egg
85 g/3 oz self-raising flour
1 tbsp cocoa powder
55 g/2 oz plain chocolate
icing sugar, for dusting

method

1 Put 8 paper baking cases in a muffin tin, or place 8 double-layer paper cases on a baking sheet.

2 Put the margarine, sugar, egg, flour and cocoa in a large bowl and, using an electric hand whisk, beat together until just smooth.

3 Spoon half of the batter into the paper cases. Using a teaspoon, make an indentation in the centre of each cake. Break the chocolate evenly into 8 squares and place a piece in each indentation, then spoon the remaining cake batter on top.

4 Bake the cupcakes in a preheated oven, 190°C/375°F/Gas Mark 5, for 20 minutes, or until well risen and springy to the touch. Leave the cupcakes for 2–3 minutes before serving warm, dusted with sifted icing sugar.

spiced chocolate muffins

ingredients

MAKES 12

100 g/3^1/$_2$ oz butter, softened
150 g/5 oz caster sugar
115 g/4 oz brown sugar
2 large eggs
150 ml/5 fl oz soured cream
5 tbsp milk
250 g/9 oz plain flour
1 tsp baking soda
2 tbsp cocoa powder
1 tsp allspice
200 g/7 oz plain chocolate
    chips

method

1 Line a 12-cup muffin tin with muffin liners.

2 Place the butter, caster sugar and brown sugar in a bowl and beat well. Beat in the eggs, soured cream and milk until thoroughly mixed. Sift the flour, baking soda, cocoa and allspice into a separate bowl and stir into the mixture. Add the chocolate chips and mix well. Divide the batter evenly between the paper liners. Bake in a preheated oven, 190°C/375°F/Gas Mark 5, for 25–30 minutes.

3 Remove from the oven and cool for 10 minutes. Place them on a wire rack to cool completely. Store in an airtight container until required.

devil's food cakes with chocolate icing

ingredients

MAKES 18

3^1/$_2$ tbsp soft margarine
115 g/4 oz brown sugar
2 large eggs
115 g/4 oz plain flour
^{1}/$_2$ tsp baking soda
25 g/1 oz cocoa powder
125 ml/4 fl oz soured cream

icing

125 g/4^1/$_2$ oz plain chocolate
2 tbsp caster sugar
150 ml/5 fl oz soured cream

chocolate curls
(optional)
100 g/3^1/$_2$ oz plain chocolate

method

1 Put 18 paper baking cases in a muffin tin, or put 18 double-layer paper cases on a baking sheet.

2 Put the margarine, sugar, eggs, flour, baking soda and cocoa in a large bowl and, using an electric hand whisk, beat together until just smooth. Using a metal spoon, fold in the soured cream. Spoon the batter into the paper cases.

3 Bake the cupcakes in a preheated oven, 180°C/350°F/Gas Mark 4, for 20 minutes, or until well risen and firm to the touch. Transfer to a wire rack to cool.

4 To make the icing, break the chocolate into a heatproof bowl. Set the bowl over a pan of gently simmering water and heat until melted, stirring occasionally. Remove from the heat and cool slightly, then whisk in the sugar and soured cream until combined. Spread the icing over the tops of the cupcakes and allow to set in the refrigerator before serving. If liked, serve decorated with chocolate curls made by shaving plain chocolate with a potato peeler.

white chocolate brownies

ingredients

MAKES 9

115 g/4 oz unsalted butter,
plus extra for greasing
225 g/8 oz white chocolate
115 g/4 oz walnut pieces
2 eggs
115 g/4 oz soft brown sugar
115 g/4 oz self-raising flour

method

1 Lightly grease an 18-cm/7-inch square cake tin with butter.

2 Coarsely chop 175 g/6 oz of chocolate and all the walnuts. Put the remaining chocolate and the butter in a heatproof bowl set over a pan of gently simmering water. When melted, stir together, then set aside to cool slightly.

3 Whisk the eggs and sugar together, then beat in the cooled chocolate mixture until well mixed. Fold in the flour, chopped chocolate and the walnuts. Turn the mixture into the prepared tin and smooth the surface.

4 Transfer the tin to a preheated oven, 180°C/350°F/Gas Mark 4, and bake for 30 minutes, or until just set. The mixture should still be a little soft in the centre. Remove from the oven and cool in the tin, then cut into 9 squares before serving.

chocolate temptations

ingredients

MAKES 24

365 g/12^1/$_2$ oz plain chocolate

6 tbsp unsalted butter, plus
    extra for greasing

1 tsp strong coffee

2 eggs

150 g/5 oz soft brown sugar

225 g/8 oz plain flour

^{1}/$_4$ tsp baking powder

pinch of salt

2 tsp almond extract

50 g/1^3/$_4$ oz Brazil nuts,
    chopped

50 g/1^3/$_4$ oz hazelnuts,
    chopped

40 g/1^1/$_2$ oz white chocolate

method

1 Put 225 g/8 oz of the plain chocolate with the butter and coffee into a heatproof bowl over a pan of simmering water and heat until the chocolate is almost melted.

2 Meanwhile, beat the eggs in a bowl until fluffy. Whisk in the sugar gradually until thick. Remove the chocolate from the heat and stir until smooth. Stir it into the egg mixture until combined.

3 Sift the flour, baking powder and salt into a bowl and stir into the chocolate mixture. Chop 85 g/3 oz of plain chocolate into pieces and stir into the dough. Stir in the almond extract and nuts.

4 Put 24 rounded dessertspoonfuls of the dough on a greased baking sheet and bake in a preheated oven, 180°C/350°F/Gas Mark 4, for 16 minutes. Transfer the cookies to a wire rack to cool. To decorate, melt the remaining chocolate (plain and white) in turn, then spoon into a piping bag and pipe lines onto the cookies.

lavender biscuits

ingredients

MAKES 12

55 g/2 oz golden caster sugar
1 tsp chopped lavender leaves
115 g/4 oz butter, softened,
    plus extra for greasing
finely grated rind of 1 lemon
175 g/6 oz plain flour

method

1 Place the sugar and lavender leaves in a food processor. Process until the lavender is very finely chopped, then add the butter and lemon rind and process until light and fluffy. Transfer to a large bowl. Sift in the flour and beat until the mixture forms a stiff dough.

2 Place the dough on a sheet of baking paper and place another sheet on top. Gently press down with a rolling pin and roll out to 3–5 mm/ $1/8$–$1/4$ inch thick. Remove the top sheet of paper and stamp out circles from the dough using a 7-cm/$2^3/4$-inch round biscuit cutter. Re-knead and re-roll the dough trimmings and stamp out more biscuits.

3 Using a spatula, carefully transfer the biscuits to a large, greased baking sheet. Prick the biscuits with a fork and bake in a preheated oven, 150°C/300°F/Gas Mark 2, for 12 minutes, or until pale golden brown. Cool on the baking sheet for 2 minutes, then transfer to a wire rack to cool completely.

fig & walnut cookies

ingredients

MAKES 20

100 g/3¹/₂ oz dried figs

225 g/8 oz unsalted butter or
    margarine, plus extra
    for greasing

125 ml/4 fl oz clear honey

4 tbsp raw brown sugar

2 eggs, beaten

pinch of salt

1 tsp allspice

1 tsp baking soda

¹/₂ tsp vanilla extract

2 tbsp dried dates, finely
    chopped

225 g/8 oz plain flour

225 g/8 oz oatmeal

25 g/1 oz walnuts, finely
    chopped

dried fig pieces, to decorate
    (optional)

method

1 Finely chop the figs. Mix the butter, honey, figs and sugar together in a large bowl. Beat the eggs into the mixture and mix thoroughly.

2 In a separate bowl, combine the salt, allspice, baking soda, vanilla extract and dates. Gradually stir them into the creamed mixture. Sift the flour into the mixture and stir well. Finally, mix in the oatmeal and walnuts.

3 Drop 20 rounded tablespoonfuls of the mixture onto 2 large greased baking sheets, spaced well apart to allow for spreading. Decorate with fig pieces, if using. Bake in a preheated oven, 180°C/350°F/Gas Mark 4, for 10–15 minutes, or until the cookies are golden brown. Remove from the oven. Transfer to a wire rack and cool completely before serving.

oat & hazelnut bites

ingredients

MAKES 30

175 g/6 oz unsalted butter or
    margarine, plus extra
    for greasing

225 g/8 oz raw brown sugar

1 egg, beaten

4 tbsp milk

1 tsp vanilla extract

$1/2$ tsp almond extract

115 g/4 oz hazelnuts

115 g/4 oz plain flour

$1^1/2$ tsp ground allspice

$1/4$ tsp baking soda

pinch of salt

225 g/8 oz oatmeal

150 g/5 oz sultanas

method

1 Cream the butter and sugar together in a mixing bowl. Blend in the egg, milk and vanilla and almond extracts until thoroughly combined. Chop the hazelnuts finely.

2 In a mixing bowl, sift the flour, allspice, baking soda and salt together. Add to the creamed mixture slowly, stirring constantly. Mix in the oatmeal, sultanas and hazelnuts.

3 Put 30 rounded tablespoonfuls of the mixture onto 2 large greased baking sheets, spaced well apart to allow for spreading. Transfer to a preheated oven, 190°C/ 375°F/ Gas Mark 5, and bake for 12–15 minutes, or until the cookies are golden brown. Remove from the oven and place on a wire rack to cool before serving.

desserts

Desserts were originally 'created' to make full use of produce that was only available for a very short season, long before sophisticated preserving equipment, such as the refrigerator and freezer, was invented! As a result, fruits, nuts, eggs and dairy produce have been transformed into the most wonderful creations, becoming ever more elegant as their role changed from necessity to sheer pleasure.

Traditional fruit pies have evolved from a simple fruit filling encased in pastry, like the Forest Fruit Pie, to some glorious variations on the theme. Toffee Apple Tart, Pear & Pecan Strudel, Pear Tarte Tatin and Blackberry Tart with Cassis Cream are delicious examples of how to make the most of nature's bounty. An alternative way to use fruit is in Peach Cobbler, with a soft batter topping, or a classic dish from France, Cherry Clafoutis – the cherries float in a creamy batter scented with vanilla extract.

Nuts are also a superb ingredient for desserts. Try Florentine Praline Tartlets, Almond Tart, Sicilian Marzipan Tart with Candied Fruit, or an old favourite, Pecan Pie. And if you can't do without chocolate, there are recipes for Chocolate Nut Strudel, Mississippi Mud Pie, Chocolate Fudge Tart, Double Chocolate Roulade and that most unusual of baked desserts – Baked Chocolate Alaska. Heaven!

toffee apple tart

ingredients

SERVES 6

butter, for greasing

flour, for sprinkling

300 g/10 oz ready-made
   shortcrust pastry

filling

1.3 kg/3 lb Pippin or other
   firm, sweet apples,
   peeled and cored

1 tsp lemon juice

3 heaped tbsp butter

100 g/3^1/$_2$ oz caster sugar

200 g/7 oz granulated sugar

75 ml/2^1/$_2$ fl oz cold water

150 ml/5 fl oz double cream,
   plus extra for serving

method

1 Lightly grease a 22-cm/9-inch loose-based fluted tart tin. Roll out the pastry on a lightly floured work surface and line the tin with it, then roll the rolling pin over the tin to trim the excess dough. Fit a piece of baking paper into the tart case and fill with dried beans. Chill in the refrigerator for 30 minutes, then bake for 10 minutes in a preheated oven, 190°C/375°F/ Gas Mark 5. Remove the beans and paper and return to the oven for 5 minutes.

2 Meanwhile, take 4 apples, cut each one into 8 pieces and toss in the lemon juice. Melt the butter in a frying pan and sauté the apple pieces until just starting to caramelize and brown on the edges. Remove from the pan and set aside to cool.

3 Slice the remaining apples thinly, put them in a pan with the caster sugar and cook for about 20 minutes, until soft. Spoon into the pastry case and arrange the reserved apple pieces on top in a circle. Bake for 30 minutes.

4 Put the granulated sugar and water in a pan and heat until the sugar dissolves. Boil to form a caramel. Remove from the heat and add the cream, stirring constantly to combine into toffee. Remove the tart from the oven, pour the toffee over the apples and chill for 1 hour. Serve with double cream.

chocolate nut strudel

ingredients

SERVES 6

150 g/5^1/$_2$ oz unsalted butter,
plus extra for greasing
225 g/8 oz mixed chopped
nuts
115 g/4 oz plain chocolate,
chopped
115 g/4 oz milk
chocolate, chopped
115 g/4 oz white chocolate,
chopped
200 g/7 oz filo pastry, thawed
if frozen
3 tbsp golden syrup
55 g/2 oz icing sugar
ice cream, to serve

method

1 Lightly grease a baking sheet with butter. Set aside 1 tablespoon of the nuts. Mix the 3 types of chocolate together.

2 Place 1 sheet of filo on a clean tea towel. Melt the butter and brush the sheet of filo with the butter, drizzle with a little syrup and sprinkle with some nuts and chocolate. Place another sheet of filo on top and repeat until you have used all the nuts and chocolate.

3 Use the tea towel to help you carefully roll up the strudel and place on the baking sheet, drizzle with a little more syrup and sprinkle with the reserved nuts. Bake in a preheated oven, 190°C/375°F/Gas Mark 5, for 20–25 minutes. If the nuts start to brown too much, cover the strudel with a sheet of foil.

4 Sprinkle the strudel with icing sugar, slice and eat warm with ice cream.

pear tarte tatin

ingredients

SERVES 6

6 tbsp butter

115 g/4 oz caster sugar

6 pears, peeled, halved
    and cored

flour, for dusting

225 g/8 oz ready-made
    puff pastry

double cream, to serve
    (optional)

method

1 Melt the butter and sugar in an ovenproof frying pan over medium heat. Stir carefully for 5 minutes until it turns to a light caramel colour. Take care because it gets very hot.

2 Remove the pan from the heat, place on a heatproof surface and arrange the pears, cut side up, in the caramel. Place one half in the centre and surround it with the others.

3 On a lightly floured work surface, roll out the dough to a round, slightly larger than the frying pan, and place it on top of the pears. Tuck the edges down into the pan.

4 Bake near the top of a preheated oven, 200°C/400°F/ Gas Mark 6, for 20–25 minutes until the pastry is well risen and golden brown. Remove from the oven and cool for 2 minutes.

5 Invert the tart onto a serving dish that is larger than the frying pan and has enough depth to take any juices that may run out. Remember that this is very hot so use a pair of thick oven gloves. Serve warm, with double cream if using.

banoffee pie

ingredients

SERVES 4

filling

3 x 400 g/14 oz cans
   sweetened
   condensed milk
4 ripe bananas
juice of $1/2$ lemon
1 tsp vanilla extract
75 g/2$3/4$ oz plain chocolate,
   grated
475 ml/16 fl oz double cream,
   whipped

biscuit base

85 g/3 oz butter, melted,
   plus extra for greasing
150 g/5$1/2$ oz digestive biscuits,
   crushed into crumbs
25 g/1 oz shelled almonds,
   toasted and ground
25 g/1 oz shelled hazelnuts,
   toasted and ground

method

1 Place the unopened cans of milk in a large pan and add enough water to cover them. Bring to a boil, then reduce the heat and simmer for 2 hours, topping up the water level to keep the cans covered. Carefully lift out the hot cans from the pan and cool.

2 Place the butter in a bowl and add the crushed digestive biscuits and ground nuts. Mix together well, then press the mixture evenly into the base and side of a greased 23-cm/9-inch tart tin. Bake in a preheated oven, 180°C/350°F/Gas Mark 4, for 10–12 minutes, then remove from the oven and cool.

3 Peel and slice the bananas and place in a bowl. Squeeze over the juice from the lemon, add the vanilla extract and mix together. Spread the banana mixture over the biscuit base in the tin, then spoon over the contents of the cooled cans of condensed milk.

4 Sprinkle over 50 g/1$3/4$ oz of the chocolate, then top with a layer of whipped cream. Sprinkle over the remaining grated chocolate and serve the pie at room temperature.

blackberry tart with cassis cream

ingredients

SERVES 6

pastry

350 g/12 oz plain flour
pinch of salt
175 g/6 oz unsalted butter
50 g/1¾ oz caster sugar
cold water

filling

750 g/1 lb 10 oz blackberries
6 tbsp golden caster sugar
1 tbsp cassis
5 tsp semolina
1 egg white

to serve

300 ml/10 fl oz double cream
1 tbsp cassis
fresh mint leaves

method

1 To make the pastry, sift the flour and salt into a large bowl and rub in the butter. Stir in the sugar and add enough cold water to bring the dough together, then wrap in clingfilm and chill for 30 minutes.

2 Meanwhile, rinse and pick over the blackberries, then put in a bowl with 4 tbsp of the sugar and the cassis, stirring to coat.

3 Roll out the dough to a large circle, handling carefully because it is quite a soft dough. Leave the edges ragged and place on a baking sheet. Sprinkle the dough with the semolina, leaving a good 6-cm/2½-inch edge. Pile the fruit into the centre and brush the edges of the dough with the egg white. Fold in the edges of the dough to overlap and enclose the fruit, making sure to press together the dough in order to close any gaps. Brush with the remaining egg white, sprinkle with the remaining sugar and bake in a preheated oven, 200°C/400°F/ Gas Mark 6, for 25 minutes.

4 To serve, whip the cream until it starts to thicken and stir in the cassis. Serve the tart hot, straight from the oven, with a good spoonful of the cassis cream and decorated with mint leaves.

peach cobbler

ingredients

SERVES 4–6

filling

6 peaches, peeled and sliced

4 tbsp caster sugar

1/2 tbsp lemon juice

1 1/2 tsp cornflour

1/2 tsp almond or vanilla extract

vanilla or pecan ice cream,
    to serve

pie topping

175 g/6 oz plain flour

115 g/4 oz caster sugar

1 1/2 tsp baking powder

1/2 tsp salt

85 g/3 oz butter, diced

1 egg

5–6 tbsp milk

method

1 Place the peaches in a 23-cm/9-inch square ovenproof dish that is also suitable for serving. Add the sugar, lemon juice, cornflour and almond extract and toss together. Bake the peaches in a preheated oven, 220°C/425°F/ Gas Mark 7, for 20 minutes.

2 Meanwhile, to make the topping, sift the flour, all but 2 tablespoons of the sugar, the baking powder and salt into a bowl. Rub in the butter with the fingertips until the mixture resembles breadcrumbs. Mix the egg and 5 tablespoons of the milk in a jug, then mix into the dry ingredients with a fork until a soft, sticky dough forms. If the dough seems too dry, stir in the extra tablespoon of milk.

3 Reduce the oven temperature to 200°C/ 400°F/Gas Mark 6. Remove the peaches from the oven and drop spoonfuls of the topping over the surface, without smoothing. Sprinkle with the remaining sugar, return to the oven and bake for a further 15 minutes, or until the topping is golden brown and firm – the topping will spread as it cooks. Serve hot or at room temperature with ice cream.

cherry clafoutis

ingredients

SERVES 6

450 g/1 lb ripe fresh cherries, pitted
100 g/3^{1}/$_2$ oz caster sugar
2 large eggs
1 egg yolk
100 g/3^{1}/$_2$ oz plain flour
pinch of salt
175 ml/6 fl oz milk
4 tbsp double cream
1 tsp vanilla extract

method

1 Lightly grease a 1.25 litre/2^{1}/$_2$ pint ovenproof serving dish or a 25-cm/10-inch quiche dish. Scatter the cherries over the bottom of the prepared dish, then place the dish on a baking sheet.

2 Using an electric mixer, whisk the sugar, eggs and the egg yolk together until blended and a pale yellow colour, scraping down the sides of the bowl as necessary.

3 Beat in the flour and salt, then slowly beat in the milk, cream and vanilla extract until a light, smooth batter forms. Pour the batter into the dish.

4 Transfer the filled dish on the baking sheet to a preheated oven, 200°C/400°F/Gas Mark 6, and bake for 45 minutes, or until the top is golden brown and the batter is set.

5 Let the pudding stand for at least 5 minutes, then serve hot, or at room temperature.

new york cheesecake

ingredients

SERVES 8–10

6 tbsp butter

200 g/7 oz digestive biscuits, crushed

sunflower oil, for brushing

400 g/14 oz cream cheese

2 large eggs

140 g/5 oz caster sugar

1$^1/_2$ tsp vanilla extract

450 ml/16 fl oz soured cream

blueberry topping

55 g/2 oz caster sugar

4 tbsp water

250 g/9 oz fresh blueberries

1 tsp arrowroot

method

1 Melt the butter in a pan over low heat. Stir in the crushed biscuits, then spread in a 20-cm/8-inch springform tin brushed with oil. Place the cream cheese, eggs, 100 g/3$^1/_2$ oz of the sugar and $^1/_2$ teaspoon of the vanilla extract in a food processor and process until smooth. Pour over the biscuit base and smooth the top. Place on a baking sheet and bake in a preheated oven, 190°C/375°F/Gas Mark 5, for 20 minutes until set. Remove from the oven and leave for 20 minutes. Leave the oven on.

2 Mix the cream with the remaining sugar and vanilla extract in a bowl. Spoon over the cheesecake. Return it to the oven for 10 minutes. Remove from the oven, cool, then chill in the refrigerator for 8 hours, or overnight.

3 To make the topping, place the sugar in a pan with 2 tablespoons of the water over low heat and stir until the sugar is dissolved. Increase the heat, add the blueberries, cover and cook for a few minutes, or until they begin to soften. Remove from the heat. Mix the arrowroot and remaining water in a bowl, add to the fruit and stir until smooth. Return to low heat. Cook until the juice thickens and turns translucent. Set aside to cool.

4 Remove the cheesecake from the tin 1 hour before serving. Spoon the fruit topping over and chill until ready to serve.

forest fruit pie

ingredients

SERVES 4

filling

225 g/8 oz blueberries

225 g/8 oz raspberries

225 g/8 oz blackberries

100 g/3^1/2 oz caster sugar

2 tbsp icing sugar,
   to decorate

whipped cream, to serve
   (optional)

pastry

225 g/8 oz plain flour, plus
   extra for dusting

25 g/1 oz ground hazelnuts

100 g/3^1/2 oz butter, cut into
   small pieces, plus extra
   for greasing

finely grated rind of 1 lemon

1 egg yolk, beaten

4 tbsp milk

method

1 Place the fruit in a pan with 3 tablespoons of the caster sugar and simmer gently, stirring frequently, for 5 minutes. Remove the pan from the heat.

2 Sift the flour into a bowl, then add the hazelnuts. Rub in the butter with the fingertips until the mixture resembles breadcrumbs, then sift in the remaining sugar. Add the lemon rind, egg yolk and 3 tablespoons of the milk and mix. Turn out onto a lightly floured work surface and knead briefly. Wrap and chill in the refrigerator for 30 minutes.

3 Grease a 20-cm/8-inch pie dish with butter. Roll out two-thirds of the pastry to a thickness of 5 mm/^{1}/4 inch and use it to line the base and side of the dish. Spoon the fruit into the pastry case. Brush the rim with water, then roll out the remaining pastry to cover the pie. Trim and crimp round the edge, then make 2 small slits in the top and decorate with 2 leaf shapes cut out from the dough trimmings. Brush all over with the remaining milk. Bake in a preheated oven, 190°C/375°F/Gas Mark 5, for 40 minutes.

4 Remove the pie from the oven, sprinkle with the icing sugar and serve with whipped cream, if using.

mississippi mud pie

ingredients

pastry

225 g/8 oz plain flour, plus
   extra for dusting
2 tbsp cocoa powder
150 g/5^1/$_2$ oz butter
2 tbsp caster sugar
1–2 tbsp cold water

filling

175 g/6 oz butter
350 g/12 oz brown sugar
4 eggs, lightly beaten
4 tbsp cocoa powder, sifted
150 g/5^1/$_2$ oz plain chocolate
300 ml/10 fl oz single cream
1 tsp chocolate extract

to decorate

425 ml/15 fl oz double cream,
   whipped
chocolate flakes and curls

method

1 To make the pastry, sift the flour and cocoa into a mixing bowl. Rub in the butter with the fingertips until the mixture resembles fine breadcrumbs. Stir in the sugar and enough cold water to mix to a soft dough. Wrap the dough and chill in the refrigerator for 15 minutes.

2 Roll out the dough on a lightly floured work surface and use to line a 23-cm/9-inch loose-based tart tin or ceramic pie dish. Line with baking paper and fill with dried beans. Bake in a preheated oven, 190°C/375°F/Gas Mark 5, for 15 minutes. Remove from the oven and take out the paper and beans. Bake the pastry case for a further 10 minutes.

3 To make the filling, beat the butter and sugar together in a bowl and gradually beat in the eggs with the cocoa. Melt the chocolate and beat it into the mixture with the single cream and the chocolate extract.

4 Reduce the oven temperature to 160°C/325°F/Gas Mark 3. Pour the mixture into the pastry case and bake for 45 minutes, or until the filling has set gently.

5 Cool the mud pie completely, then transfer it to a serving plate, if you like. Cover with the whipped cream. Decorate the pie with chocolate flakes and curls and then chill until ready to serve.

florentine praline tartlets

ingredients

MAKES 6 TARTLETS

praline
100 g/3¹/2 oz granulated
    sugar
3 tbsp water
50 g/1³/4 oz slivered almonds
butter

pastry
125 g/4¹/2 oz plain flour
pinch of salt
75 g/2¹/2 oz cold butter,
    cut into pieces
1 tsp icing sugar
cold water

frangipane
75 g/2¹/2 oz butter
2 eggs
75 g/2¹/2 oz caster sugar
2 tbsp plain flour
115 g/4 oz ground almonds

topping
8 natural candied cherries,
    chopped
2 tbsp mixed candied peel,
    chopped
100 g/3¹/2 oz plain chocolate,
    chopped

method

1 To make the praline, put the sugar and water in a pan and dissolve the sugar over low heat. Do not stir the sugar, just let it boil for 10 minutes, until it turns to caramel, then stir in the nuts and turn out onto buttered foil. Set aside to cool and harden. When cold break up the praline and chop into smallish pieces.

2 Grease 6 x 9-cm/3¹/2-inch loose-based fluted tart tins. Sift the flour and salt into a food processor, add the butter and process until the mixture resembles fine breadcrumbs. Add the sugar and a little cold water and pulse to bring the dough together. Turn out onto a floured work surface and divide into 6 pieces. Roll out each piece and use to line the tart tins. Roll the rolling pin over the tins to trim the excess dough. Freeze for 30 minutes.

3 Meanwhile, make the frangipane. Melt the butter and beat the eggs and sugar together. Stir the melted butter into the egg and sugar mixture, then add the flour and almonds.

4 Bake the tart cases blind, straight from the freezer, for 10 minutes in a preheated oven, 200°C/400°F/Gas Mark 6. Divide the frangipane between the tart cases and return to the oven for 8–10 minutes. Meanwhile, mix the cherries, peel, chocolate and praline together. Divide between the tarts while they are still hot so that some of the chocolate melts. Serve cold.

chocolate fudge tart

ingredients

SERVES 6

flour, for sprinkling
350 g/12 oz ready-made
    shortcrust pastry
icing sugar, for dusting

filling

140 g/5 oz plain chocolate,
    finely chopped
175 g/6 oz butter, diced
350 g/12 oz golden
    granulated sugar
100 g/3¹/₂ oz plain flour
¹/₂ tsp vanilla extract
6 eggs, beaten

to decorate

150 ml/5 fl oz whipped cream
ground cinnamon

method

1 Roll out the pastry on a lightly floured work surface and use to line a 20-cm/8-inch deep loose-based tart tin. Prick the dough base lightly with a fork, then line with foil and fill with dried beans. Bake in a preheated oven, 200°C/400°F/Gas Mark 6, for 12–15 minutes, or until the dough no longer looks raw. Remove the beans and foil and bake for a further 10 minutes, or until the dough is firm. Set aside to cool. Reduce the oven temperature to 180°C/350°F/Gas Mark 4.

2 To make the filling, place the chocolate and butter in a heatproof bowl and set over a pan of gently simmering water until melted. Stir until smooth, then remove from the heat and cool. Place the sugar, flour, vanilla extract and eggs in a separate bowl and whisk until well blended. Stir in the butter and chocolate mixture.

3 Pour the filling into the pastry case and bake in the oven for 50 minutes, or until the filling is just set. Transfer to a wire rack to cool completely. Dust with icing sugar before serving with whipped cream sprinkled lightly with cinnamon.

almond tart

ingredients

SERVES 8

280 g/10 oz plain flour, plus
    extra for dusting
150 g/5^1/$_2$ oz caster sugar
1 tsp finely grated lemon rind
pinch of salt
150 g/5^1/$_2$ oz unsalted butter,
    chilled and cut into
      small dice
1 medium egg, beaten lightly
1 tbsp chilled water

filling

175 g/6 oz unsalted butter,
    at room temperature
175 g/6 oz caster sugar
3 large eggs
175 g/6 oz finely
    ground almonds
2 tsp plain flour
1 tbsp finely grated orange rind
^{1}/$_2$ tsp almond extract
icing sugar, to decorate
soured cream (optional),
    to serve

method

1 To make the pastry, put the flour, sugar, lemon rind and salt in a bowl. Rub or cut in the butter until the mixture resembles fine breadcrumbs. Combine the egg and water, then slowly pour into the flour, stirring with a fork until a coarse mass forms. Shape into a ball and chill for at least 1 hour.

2 Roll out the pastry on a lightly floured work surface until 3 mm/^{1}/$_8$ inch thick. Use to line a greased 25-cm/10-inch tart tin. Return to the refrigerator for 15 minutes, then cover the pastry case with foil and fill with dried beans. Place in a preheated oven, 220°C/425°F/Gas Mark 7, and bake for 12 minutes. Remove the dried beans and foil and return the pastry case to the oven for 4 minutes. Remove from the oven and reduce the oven temperature to 200°C/400°F/Gas Mark 6.

3 Meanwhile, make the filling. Beat the butter and sugar until creamy. Beat in the eggs, 1 at a time. Add the almonds, flour, orange rind and almond extract and beat until blended.

4 Spoon the filling into the pastry case and smooth the surface. Bake for 30–35 minutes until the top is golden and the tip of a knife inserted in the centre comes out clean. Cool completely on a wire rack, then dust with sifted icing sugar. Serve with a spoonful of soured cream, if using.

sicilian marzipan tart with candied fruit

ingredients

SERVES 6

pastry

125 g/4^1/$_2$ oz plain flour, plus
  extra for dusting
pinch of salt
75 g/2^1/$_2$ oz cold butter,
  cut into pieces
cold water

filling

300 g/10^1/$_2$ oz marzipan
175 g/6 oz ground almonds
150 g/5^1/$_2$ oz unsalted butter
100 g/3^1/$_2$ oz caster sugar
55 g/2 oz plain flour
2 eggs
55 g/2 oz sultanas
55 g/2 oz mixed candied
  peel, chopped
55 g/2 oz natural candied
  cherries, halved
55 g/2 oz flaked almonds

method

1 Lightly grease a 22-cm/9-inch loose-based fluted tart tin. Sift the flour and salt into a food processor, add the butter and process until the mixture resembles fine breadcrumbs. Add just enough cold water to bring the dough together. Turn out onto a work surface dusted with more flour and roll out the dough 8 cm/3¼ inches larger than the tin. Lift the dough into the tin and press to fit. Roll the rolling pin over the tin to trim the excess dough. Fit a piece of baking paper into the tart case and fill with dried beans.

2 Chill for 30 minutes, then bake for 10 minutes in a preheated oven, 190°C/375°F/Gas Mark 5. Remove the beans and paper and bake for a further 5 minutes. Lower the temperature to 180°C/350°F/Gas Mark 4. Grate the marzipan straight onto the base of the warm pastry.

3 Put the ground almonds, butter and sugar in a food processor and pulse until smooth. Add 1 tbsp flour and 1 of the eggs and blend, then add another 1 tbsp flour and the other egg and blend. Finally add the remaining flour. Scoop the mixture into a bowl and stir in the sultanas, peel and cherries. Spoon the mixture over the marzipan, sprinkle with the flaked almonds and bake for 40 minutes. Serve cold.

baked chocolate alaska

ingredients

SERVES 4

butter, for greasing

2 eggs

175 g/6 oz caster sugar,
    plus 4 tbsp

4 tbsp plain flour

2 tbsp cocoa powder

3 egg whites

1 litre/1¾ pints good-quality
    chocolate ice cream

method

1 Grease an 18-cm/7-inch round cake tin and line the base with baking paper.

2 Whisk the eggs and the 4 tablespoons of sugar in a mixing bowl until very thick and pale. Sift the flour and cocoa together and carefully fold in.

3 Pour into the prepared tin and bake in a preheated oven, 220°C/425°F/Gas Mark 7, for 7 minutes, or until springy to the touch. Turn out and transfer to a wire rack to cool completely.

4 Whisk the egg whites in a clean, greasefree bowl until soft peaks form. Gradually add the remaining sugar, whisking until you have a thick, glossy meringue. Place the sponge on a baking sheet. Soften the ice cream in the refrigerator and pile it onto the centre to form a dome.

5 Pipe or spread the meringue over the ice cream, making sure it is completely enclosed. (At this point the dessert can be frozen, if wished.) Return to the oven for 5 minutes, until the meringue is a light golden brown. Serve at once.

pecan pie

ingredients

SERVES 8

pastry

250 g/9 oz plain flour

pinch of salt

115 g/4 oz butter, cut into
    small pieces

1 tbsp lard or vegetable
    shortening, cut into
    small pieces

55 g/2 oz golden caster sugar

6 tbsp cold milk

filling

3 eggs

250 g/8 oz muscovado sugar

1 tsp vanilla extract

pinch of salt

85 g/3 oz butter, melted

3 tbsp golden syrup

3 tbsp molasses

350 g/12 oz shelled pecans,
    roughly chopped

pecan halves, to decorate

whipped cream or vanilla ice
    cream, to serve

method

1 To make the pastry, sift the flour and salt into a mixing bowl and rub in the butter and lard with the fingertips until the mixture resembles fine breadcrumbs. Work in the caster sugar and add the milk. Work the mixture into a soft dough. Wrap the dough and chill in the refrigerator for 30 minutes.

2 Roll out the pastry and use it to line a 23–25-cm/9–10 inch tart tin. Trim off the excess by running the rolling pin over the top of the tart tin. Line with baking paper and fill with dried beans. Bake in a preheated oven, 200°C/400°F/Gas Mark 6, for 20 minutes. Take out of the oven and remove the paper and dried beans. Reduce the oven temperature to 180°C/350°F/Gas Mark 4. Place a baking sheet in the oven.

3 To make the filling, place the eggs in a bowl and beat lightly. Beat in the muscovado sugar, vanilla extract and salt. Stir in the butter, syrup, molasses and chopped nuts. Pour into the pastry case and decorate with the pecan halves.

4 Place on the heated baking sheet and bake in the oven for 35-40 minutes until the filling is set. Serve warm or at room temperature with whipped cream or vanilla ice cream.

lemon meringue pie

ingredients

SERVES 8–10

butter, for greasing

plain flour, for dusting

250 g/9 oz ready-made
   shortcrust pastry,
   thawed if frozen

3 tbsp cornflour

85 g/3 oz caster sugar

grated rind of 3 lemons

300 ml/10 fl oz cold water

150 ml/5 fl oz lemon juice

3 egg yolks

55 g/2 oz unsalted butter,
   cut into small cubes

meringue

3 egg whites

175 g/6 oz caster sugar

1 tsp golden granulated sugar

method

1 Grease a 25-cm/10-inch fluted tart tin. On a lightly floured work surface, roll out the pastry and ease it into the tin, rolling off the excess. Prick the bottom of the tart case and chill, uncovered, for 30 minutes. Line with baking paper and fill with dried beans. Bake on a preheated baking sheet in a preheated oven, 200ºC/400ºF/Gas Mark 6, for 15 minutes. Remove the beans and paper and return to the oven for 10 minutes. Remove and reduce the temperature to 150ºC/300ºF/Gas Mark 2.

2 Put the cornflour, sugar and lemon rind into a pan. Blend in a little of the water to make a smooth paste. Gradually add the remaining water and the lemon juice. Bring to a boil over medium heat, stirring continuously. Simmer gently for 1 minute until smooth and glossy. Remove from the heat. Beat in the egg yolks, 1 at a time, then the butter. Place the pan in a bowl of cold water to cool the filling, then spoon it into the tart case.

3 To make the meringue, whisk the egg whites until thick and in soft peaks. Gradually add the caster sugar, whisking well with each addition. Spoon the meringue over the filling to cover it completely. Swirl the meringue into peaks and sprinkle with granulated sugar. Bake for 20–30 minutes until the meringue is crispy and pale gold (the centre should still be soft). Cool slightly before serving.

double chocolate roulade

ingredients

SERVES 8

4 eggs, separated

115 g/4 oz golden caster
    sugar

115 g/4 oz plain chocolate,
    melted and cooled

1 tsp instant coffee granules,
    dissolved in 2 tbsp hot
    water, cooled

icing sugar, to decorate

cocoa powder, for dusting

fresh raspberries, to serve

filling

250 ml/9 fl oz whipping
    cream

140 g/5 oz white chocolate,
    broken into pieces

3 tbsp Tia Maria

method

1 Line a 23 x 33-cm/9 x 13-inch Swiss roll tin with nonstick baking paper. Whisk the egg yolks and sugar in a bowl until pale and mousse-like. Fold in the chocolate, then the coffee. Place the egg whites in a clean bowl and whisk until stiff but not dry. Stir a little of the egg whites into the chocolate mixture, then fold in the remainder. Pour into the tin and bake in a preheated oven, 180°C/350°F/ Gas Mark 4, for 15–20 minutes, or until firm. Cover with a damp tea towel and let stand in the tin for 8 hours, or overnight.

2 Meanwhile, make the filling. Heat the cream until almost boiling. Place the chocolate in a food processor and chop coarsely. With the motor running, pour the cream through the feed tube. Process until smooth. Stir in the Tia Maria. Transfer to a bowl and cool. Chill for 8 hours, or overnight.

3 To assemble the roulade, whip the chocolate cream until soft peaks form. Cut a sheet of waxed paper larger than the roulade, place on a work surface and sift icing sugar over it. Turn the roulade out onto the paper. Peel away the lining paper. Spread the chocolate cream over the roulade and roll up from the short side nearest to you. Transfer to a dish, seam-side down. Chill for 2 hours, then dust with cocoa. Serve with raspberries.

baking
with yeast

Baking with yeast seems to hold terrors for those who have never tried it, and yet it is really easy, especially now that easy-blend dried yeast has largely superseded the use of fresh yeast. Yeast cooking needs a little planning because of the time required for the dough to rise, but there is absolutely nothing to beat the aroma of fresh bread wafting through your home, so the wait is more than worth it.

Sweet breads are delicious for breakfast or brunch, or with coffee or tea at any time of day. Life will never be the same once you've mastered those flaky, buttery French specialities, Croissants and Pains au Chocolat, or the slightly less messy-to-eat brioche – we've selected a delicious Orange & Raisin Brioche for you to try. Cinnamon Swirls and Crown Loaf are fun to eat, too – you can bite into them tidily, or unroll them to pull out the fruity bits of filling!

Savoury breads are the perfect accompaniment to soups, salads, and main meals. Both sweet and savoury breads are great for making sandwiches – try Apricot & Walnut Bread with a filling of cream cheese, or Olive & Sun-dried Tomato Bread packed with your favourite cold cuts and some watercress. And if you love pizza, there's a recipe for a basic Cheese & Tomato Pizza – you can dress it up all you like.

fresh croissants

ingredients

MAKES 12 CROISSANTS

500 g/1 lb 2 oz white bread
  flour, plus extra for dusting
40 g/1$^{1}/_2$ oz caster sugar
1 tsp salt
2 tsp easy-blend dried yeast
300 ml/10 fl oz milk, heated
  until just warm to the
  touch
300 g/10$^{1}/_2$ oz butter,
  softened, flattened with
  a rolling pin between
  2 sheets of waxed paper
  to form a rectangle
  5 mm/$^{1}/_4$ inch thick, then
  chilled in the refrigerator,
  plus extra for greasing
1 egg, lightly beaten with
  1 tbsp milk, to glaze
jam, to serve (optional)

you will need

a cardboard triangular
  template, base 18 cm/
  7 inches and sides
  20 cm/8 inches

method

1 Stir the dry ingredients in a large bowl, make a well in the centre and add the milk. Mix to a soft dough, adding more milk if too dry. Knead on a lightly floured work surface for 5–10 minutes, or until smooth and elastic. Let rise in a large, greased bowl, covered, in a warm place until doubled in size.

2 Knead the dough for 1 minute. Let the butter soften slightly. Roll out the dough on a well-floured work surface to 46 x 15 cms/18 x 6 inches. Place the butter in the centre. Then with the short end of the dough towards you, fold the top third down towards the centre, then fold the bottom third up and squeeze the edges together gently. Rotate so that the fold is to your left and the top flap towards your right. Roll out to a rectangle and fold again. If the butter feels soft, wrap the dough in clingfilm and chill. Repeat the rolling process twice more. Cut the dough in half. Roll out one half into a triangle 5 mm/$^{1}/_4$ inch thick (keep the other half refrigerated). Use the cardboard template to cut out the croissants.

3 Brush the triangles lightly with the glaze. Roll into croissant shapes, starting at the base and tucking under the point. Brush again with the glaze and place on an ungreased baking sheet. Let double in size, then bake in a preheated oven, 200°C/400°F/Gas Mark 6, for 15–20 minutes until golden. Serve with jam, if liked.

orange & raisin brioches

ingredients

MAKES 12

55 g/2 oz butter, melted, plus
    extra for greasing
225 g/8 oz strong white bread
    flour, plus extra for dusting
1/2 tsp salt
2 tsp easy-blend dried yeast
1 tbsp golden caster sugar
55 g/2 oz raisins
grated rind of 1 orange
2 tbsp tepid water
2 eggs, beaten
vegetable oil, for brushing
1 beaten egg, for glazing
butter, to serve (optional)

method

1 Grease 12 individual brioche moulds. Sift the flour and salt into a warmed bowl and stir in the yeast, sugar, raisins and orange rind. Make a well in the centre. In a separate bowl, mix together the water, eggs and melted butter and pour into the dry ingredients. Beat vigorously to make a soft dough. Turn out onto a lightly floured work surface and knead for 5 minutes, or until smooth and elastic. Brush a clean bowl with oil. Place the dough in the bowl, cover with clingfilm and let stand in a warm place for 1 hour, or until doubled in size.

2 Turn out onto a floured work surface, knead lightly for 1 minute, then roll into a rope shape. Cut into 12 equal pieces. Shape three-quarters of each piece into a ball and place in the prepared moulds. With a floured finger, press a hole in the centre of each. Shape the remaining pieces of dough into little plugs and press into the holes, flattening the top slightly.

3 Place the moulds on a baking sheet, cover lightly with oiled clingfilm and let stand in a warm place for 1 hour, until the dough comes almost to the top.

4 Brush the brioches with beaten egg and bake in a preheated oven, 220°C/425°F/Gas Mark 7, for 15 minutes, or until golden brown. Serve warm with butter, if you like.

pains au chocolat

ingredients

MAKES 8

100 g/3^1/$_2$ oz butter, plus
    extra for greasing
250 g/9 oz white bread flour,
    plus extra for dusting
1 tsp salt
2 tsp easy-blend dried yeast
175 ml/6 fl oz milk
2 tbsp golden caster sugar
1 tbsp oil, plus extra for
    brushing
115 g/4 oz plain chocolate,
    coarsely chopped

glaze

1 egg yolk
2 tbsp milk

method

1 Grease a baking sheet. Sift the flour and salt into a bowl and stir in the yeast. Make a well in the centre. Heat the milk in a pan until tepid. Add the sugar and oil and stir until the sugar has dissolved. Stir into the flour and mix well. Turn the dough out onto a lightly floured work surface and knead until smooth, then place in an oiled bowl. Cover and let rise in a warm place for 2–3 hours, or until doubled in size.

2 Knead on a floured work surface and roll into a rectangle 3 times as long as it is wide. Divide the butter into thirds. Dot one portion over the top two-thirds of the dough, leaving a 1-cm/ ½-inch margin round the edges. Fold the lower third up and the top third down. Seal the edges. Give the dough a half-turn. Roll into a rectangle. Repeat the process twice, then fold in half. Put into an oiled plastic bag. Chill for 1 hour.

3 Cut the dough in half and roll out into 2 rectangles of 30 x 15 cm/12 x 6 inches. Cut each half into 4 rectangles of 15 x 7.5 cm/ 6 x 3 inches. Sprinkle chocolate along one short end of each and roll up. Place on the baking sheet in a warm place for 2–3 hours, or until doubled in size. To glaze, mix the egg yolk and milk and brush over the rolls. Bake in a preheated oven, 220°C/425°F/Gas Mark 7, for 15–20 minutes, or until golden and well risen.

chocolate bread

ingredients

MAKES 1 LOAF

butter, for greasing

450 g/1 lb strong white bread
flour, plus extra for dusting

25 g/1 oz cocoa powder

1 tsp salt

1 sachet easy-blend dried
yeast

2 tbsp brown sugar

1 tbsp corn oil

300 ml/10 fl oz lukewarm
water

butter, to serve

method

1 Lightly grease a 900-g/2-lb loaf tin with a little butter. Sift the flour and cocoa into a large bowl. Stir in the salt, yeast and brown sugar. Pour in the oil and water and mix together to form a dough.

2 Knead the dough on a lightly floured work surface for 5 minutes. Alternatively, use an electric mixer with a dough hook. Place the dough in a greased bowl, cover and let rise in a warm place for 1 hour, or until doubled in size.

3 Punch down the dough and shape it into a loaf. Place the dough in the tin, cover and let stand in a warm place for a further 30 minutes.

4 Bake the bread in a preheated oven, 200°C/400°F/Gas Mark 6, for 25–30 minutes, or until a hollow sound is heard when the bottom of the bread is tapped. Transfer the bread to a wire rack and cool completely. Cut into slices and serve with butter.

stollen

ingredients

SERVES 10

85 g/3 oz currants

55 g/2 oz raisins

2 tbsp chopped candied peel

55 g/2 oz candied cherries,
   rinsed, dried and
   quartered

2 tbsp rum

55 g/2 oz butter

175 ml/6 fl oz milk

2 tbsp golden caster sugar

375 g/13 oz strong white
   bread flour, plus extra
   for dusting

1/2 tsp ground nutmeg

1/2 tsp ground cinnamon

seeds from 3 cardamoms

2 tsp easy-blend dried yeast

finely grated rind of 1 lemon

1 egg, beaten

40 g/1 1/2 oz flaked almonds

vegetable oil, for brushing

175 g/6 oz marzipan

melted butter, for brushing

sifted icing sugar,
   for dredging

method

1 Place the currants, raisins, peel and cherries in a bowl, stir in the rum and set aside. Place the butter, milk and sugar in a pan over low heat and stir until the sugar dissolves and the butter melts. Cool until lukewarm. Sift the flour, nutmeg and cinnamon into a bowl. Crush the cardamom seeds and add them. Stir in the yeast. Make a well in the centre, stir in the milk mixture, lemon rind and egg and beat into a dough.

2 Turn the dough out onto a floured work surface and knead for 5 minutes. Knead in the soaked fruit and the almonds. Transfer to a clean, oiled bowl. Cover with clingfilm and let stand in a warm place for up to 3 hours, or until doubled in size. Turn out onto a floured work surface, knead for 1–2 minutes, then roll out to a 25-cm/ 10-inch square.

3 Roll the marzipan into a sausage shorter than the length of the dough. Place in the centre. Fold the dough over the marzipan, overlapping it. Seal the ends. Place seam-side down on a greased baking sheet, cover with oiled clingfilm and let stand in a warm place for up to 2 hours, or until doubled in size. Preheat the oven to 190°C/375°F/Gas Mark 5. Bake for 40 minutes, or until golden and hollow sounding when tapped. Brush with melted butter, dredge with icing sugar and cool on a wire rack.

cinnamon swirls

ingredients

SERVES 12

2 tbsp butter, cut into small
　　pieces, plus extra
　　for greasing
225 g/8 oz strong white
　　bread flour
$^1/_2$ tsp salt
1 sachet easy-blend dried
　　yeast
1 egg, beaten
125 ml/4 fl oz warm milk
2 tbsp maple syrup

filling

4 tbsp butter, softened
2 tsp ground cinnamon
50 g/1$^3/_4$ oz brown sugar
50 g/1$^3/_4$ oz currants

method

1 Grease a 23-cm/9-inch square cake tin. Sift the flour and salt into a bowl. Stir in the yeast. Rub in the butter with your fingertips until the mixture resembles fine breadcrumbs. Add the egg and milk and mix to form a dough. Place in a greased bowl, cover and let stand in a warm place for 40 minutes, or until doubled in size.

2 Knead the dough lightly for 1 minute to punch it down, then roll out on a lightly floured work surface to form a rectangle measuring 30 x 23 cm/12 x 9 inches.

3 To make the filling, beat the butter, cinnamon and brown sugar together until the mixture is light and fluffy. Spread the filling over the dough, leaving a 2.5-cm/1-inch border all round. Sprinkle over the currants.

4 Carefully roll up the dough like a Swiss roll, starting at a long edge, and press down to seal. Using a sharp knife, cut the roll into 12 slices. Place them in the prepared tin, cover and let stand for 30 minutes.

5 Bake the swirls in a preheated oven, 190°C/ 375°F/Gas Mark 5, for 20–30 minutes, or until well risen. Brush the swirls with the syrup and cool slightly before serving warm.

crown loaf

ingredients

MAKES 1 LOAF

2 tbsp butter, diced, plus
 extra for greasing
225 g/8 oz strong white bread
 flour, plus extra for dusting
$^1/_2$ tsp salt
1 sachet easy-blend
 dried yeast
125 ml/4 fl oz lukewarm milk
1 egg, beaten lightly

filling

4 tbsp butter, softened
50 g/1$^3/_4$ oz brown sugar
2 tbsp chopped hazelnuts
1 tbsp chopped preserved
 ginger
50 g/1$^3/_4$ oz candied peel
1 tbsp rum or brandy

icing

100 g/3$^1/_2$ oz icing sugar
2 tbsp lemon juice

method

1 Grease a baking sheet with a little butter. Sift the flour and salt into a large mixing bowl. Stir in the yeast. Rub in the butter with your fingertips. Add the milk and egg and bring together with your fingers to form a dough.

2 Place the dough in a greased bowl, cover and let stand in a warm place for about 40 minutes, until doubled in size. Punch down the dough lightly for 1 minute, then roll out into a rectangle measuring 30 x 23 cm/ 12 x 9 inches.

3 To make the filling, cream the butter and sugar together in a large bowl until light and fluffy. Stir in the hazelnuts, ginger, candied peel and rum or brandy. Spread the filling over the dough, leaving a 2.5-cm/1-inch border around the edges.

4 Roll up the dough, starting from one of the long edges, into a sausage shape. Cut into slices at 5-cm/2-inch intervals and place the slices in a circle on the baking sheet, sides just touching. Cover and stand in a warm place to rise for 30 minutes.

5 Bake in a preheated oven, 190°C/375°F/Gas Mark 5, for 20–30 minutes or until golden. Meanwhile, mix the icing sugar with enough lemon juice to form a thin icing. Cool the loaf slightly before drizzling with icing. Allow the icing to set slightly before serving.

date & honey loaf

ingredients

SERVES 10

butter, for greasing

250 g/9 oz strong white bread
 flour, plus extra for dusting

75 g/2¾ oz strong brown
 bread flour

½ tsp salt

1 sachet easy-blend dried
 yeast

200 ml/7 fl oz lukewarm water

3 tbsp corn oil

3 tbsp honey

75 g/2¾ oz dried dates,
 chopped

2 tbsp sesame seeds

method

1 Grease a 900-g/2-lb loaf tin with butter. Sift the white and brown flours into a large bowl and stir in the salt and yeast. Pour in the water, oil and honey and mix to form a dough.

2 Place the dough on a lightly floured work surface and knead for 5 minutes, or until smooth, then place in a greased bowl. Cover and let rise in a warm place for 1 hour, or until doubled in size.

3 Knead in the dates and the sesame seeds. Shape the dough and place in the prepared loaf tin. Cover and let stand in a warm place for a further 30 minutes, or until springy to the touch.

4 Bake the loaf in a preheated oven, 220°C/425°F/Gas Mark 7, for 30 minutes, or until the bottom of the loaf sounds hollow when tapped. Transfer to a wire rack and cool completely. Serve cut into thick slices.

banana & orange bread

ingredients

MAKES 1 MEDIUM LOAF

500 g/1 lb 2 oz white bread
   flour, plus an extra 1–2
   tbsp for sticky dough
1 tsp salt
1 tsp easy-blend dried yeast
3 tbsp butter, diced
2 medium ripe bananas
   or 1 large ripe banana,
   peeled and mashed
3 tbsp runny honey
4 tbsp orange juice
200 ml/7 fl oz hand-hot
   buttermilk
milk, to glaze (optional)
vegetable oil, for brushing

method

1 Place the flour, salt and yeast in a large bowl. Rub in the butter and add the mashed bananas and honey. Make a well in the centre and gradually work in the orange juice and buttermilk to make a smooth dough.

2 Turn the dough out onto a lightly floured work surface and knead for 5–7 minutes, or until the dough is smooth and elastic. If the dough looks very sticky, add a little more white bread flour. (The stickiness depends on the ripeness and size of the bananas.) Place the dough in an oiled bowl, cover with clingfilm and leave in a warm place to rise for 1 hour, or until it has doubled in size.

3 Oil a 900-g/2-lb loaf tin. Turn the dough out onto a lightly floured work surface and knead for 1 minute until smooth. Shape the dough the length of the tin and three times the width. Fold the dough into three lengthways and place it in the tin with the join underneath. Cover and let stand in a warm place for 30 minutes until it has risen above the tin.

4 Just before baking, brush the milk over the loaf to glaze, if using. Bake in a preheated oven, 220°C/425°F/Gas Mark 7, for 30 minutes, or until firm and golden brown. Test that the loaf is cooked by tapping it on the bottom – it should sound hollow. Transfer to a wire rack to cool completely before serving.

mango twist bread

ingredients

MAKES 1 LOAF

3 tbsp butter, diced, plus
    extra for greasing
450 g/1 lb strong white bread
    flour, plus extra for dusting
1 tsp salt
1 sachet easy-blend
    dried yeast
1 tsp ground ginger
50 g/1³/4 oz brown sugar
1 small mango, peeled, pitted
    and blended to a purée
250 ml/9 fl oz lukewarm water
2 tbsp honey
125 g/4¹/2 oz sultanas
1 egg, beaten lightly
icing sugar, for dusting

method

1 Grease a baking sheet with a little butter. Sift the flour and salt into a mixing bowl, stir in the dry yeast, ginger and brown sugar and rub in the butter with your fingertips until the mixture resembles breadcrumbs.

2 Stir in the mango purée, lukewarm water and honey and bring together to form a dough.

3 Place the dough on a lightly floured work surface. Knead for about 5 minutes, until smooth. Alternatively, use an electric mixer with a dough hook. Place the dough in a greased bowl, cover and let rise in a warm place for about 1 hour, until it has doubled in size.

4 Knead in the sultanas and shape the dough into 2 rope shapes, each 25 cm/10 inches long. Carefully twist the 2 pieces together and pinch the ends to seal. Place the dough on the baking sheet, cover and let stand in a warm place for a further 40 minutes.

5 Brush the loaf with the egg. Bake in a preheated oven, 220°C/425°F/Gas Mark 7, for 30 minutes, or until golden. Cool on a wire rack and dust with icing sugar before serving.

apricot & walnut bread

ingredients

SERVES 12

55 g/2 oz butter, plus extra
    for greasing
350 g/12 oz strong white
    bread flour, plus extra
    for dusting
$^1/_2$ tsp salt
1 tsp golden caster sugar
2 tsp easy-blend dried yeast
115 g/4 oz no-soak dried
    apricots, chopped
55 g/2 oz chopped walnuts
150 ml/5 fl oz tepid milk
75 ml/2$^1/_2$ fl oz tepid water
1 egg, beaten
vegetable oil, for brushing

topping

85 g/3 oz icing sugar
walnut halves

method

1 Grease and flour a baking sheet. Sift the flour and salt into a warmed bowl and stir in the sugar and yeast. Rub in the butter and add the chopped apricots and walnuts. Make a well in the centre. In a separate bowl, mix together the milk, water and egg. Pour into the dry ingredients and mix to a soft dough. Turn out onto a floured work surface and knead for 10 minutes, or until smooth. Place the dough in a clean bowl brushed with oil, cover with oiled clingfilm and let stand in a warm place for 2–3 hours, or until doubled in size.

2 Turn the dough out onto a floured work surface and knead lightly for 1 minute. Divide into 5 equal pieces and roll each piece into a rope 30 cm/12 inches long. Braid 3 ropes together, pinching the ends to seal, and place on the prepared baking sheet. Twist the remaining 2 ropes together and place on top. Cover lightly with oiled clingfilm and let stand in a warm place for 1–2 hours, or until doubled in size.

3 Bake the bread in a preheated oven, 220°C/425°F/Gas Mark 7, for 10 minutes, then reduce the heat to 190°C/375°F/Gas Mark 5 and bake for a further 20 minutes. Transfer to a wire rack to cool. To make the topping, sift the icing sugar into a bowl, stir in enough water to make a thin icing and drizzle over the loaf. Decorate with walnuts.

crusty white bread

ingredients

MAKES 1 MEDIUM LOAF

1 egg

1 egg yolk

hand-hot water, as required

500 g/1 lb 2 oz white bread
   flour, plus extra for dusting

$1^1/_2$ tsp salt

2 tsp sugar

1 tsp easy-blend dried yeast

2 tbsp butter, diced

vegetable oil, for brushing

method

1 Place the egg and egg yolk in a jug and beat lightly to mix. Add enough hand-hot water to make up to 300 ml/10 fl oz. Stir well.

2 Place the flour, salt, sugar and yeast in a large bowl. Add the butter and rub it in with your fingertips until the mixture resembles breadcrumbs. Make a well in the centre, add the egg mixture and work to a smooth dough.

3 Turn the dough out onto a lightly floured work surface and knead for 10 minutes, or until the dough is smooth and elastic. Place the dough in an oiled bowl, cover with clingfilm and leave in a warm place to rise for 1 hour, or until it has doubled in size.

4 Oil a 900-g/2-lb loaf tin. Turn the dough out onto a lightly floured work surface and knead for 1 minute until smooth. Shape the dough the length of the tin and three times the width. Fold the dough into three lengthways and place it in the tin with the join underneath. Cover and leave in a warm place for 30 minutes until it has risen above the tin.

5 Bake in a preheated oven, 220°C/425°F/ Gas Mark 7, for 30 minutes, or until firm and golden brown. Test that the loaf is cooked by tapping it on the bottom – it should sound hollow. Transfer to a wire rack to cool completely.

olive & sun-dried tomato bread

ingredients

SERVES 4

400 g/14 oz plain flour, plus
extra for dusting

1 tsp salt

1 sachet easy-blend dried
yeast

1 tsp brown sugar

1 tbsp chopped fresh thyme

200 ml/7 fl oz warm water
(heated to 50°C/122°F)

4 tbsp olive oil, plus
extra for oiling

50 g/1³/4 oz black olives,
pitted and sliced

50 g/1³/4 oz green olives,
pitted and sliced

100 g/3¹/2 oz sun-dried
tomatoes in oil, drained
and sliced

1 egg yolk, beaten

method

1 Place the flour, salt and yeast in a bowl and mix together, then stir in the sugar and thyme. Make a well in the centre. Slowly stir in enough water and oil to make a dough. Mix in the olives and sun-dried tomatoes. Knead the dough for 5 minutes, then form it into a ball. Brush a bowl with oil, add the dough and cover with clingfilm. Let rise in a warm place for about 1¹/2 hours, or until the dough has doubled in size.

2 Dust a baking sheet with flour. Knead the dough lightly, then cut into two halves and shape into ovals or circles. Place them on the baking sheet, cover with clingfilm and let rise again in a warm place for 45 minutes, or until they have doubled in size.

3 Make 3 shallow diagonal cuts on the top of each piece of dough. Brush with the egg. Bake in a preheated oven, 200°C/400°F/ Gas Mark 6, for 40 minutes, or until cooked through – they should be golden on top and sound hollow when tapped on the bottom. Transfer to wire racks to cool. Store in an airtight container for up to 3 days.

black olive focaccia

ingredients

SERVES 12

500 g/1 lb 2 oz strong white
bread flour, plus extra
for dusting

1 tsp salt

2 tsp easy-blend dried yeast

350 ml/12 fl oz tepid water

6 tbsp extra-virgin olive oil,
plus extra for brushing

115 g/4 oz pitted black olives,
coarsely chopped

1 tsp rock salt

method

1 Sift the flour and salt into a warmed bowl and stir in the yeast. Pour in the water and 2 tablespoons of the olive oil and mix to a soft dough. Knead the dough on a lightly floured work surface for 5–10 minutes, or until it becomes smooth and elastic. Transfer it to a clean, warmed, oiled bowl and cover with clingfilm. Let stand in a warm place for 1 hour, or until the dough has doubled in size.

2 Brush 2 baking sheets with oil. Punch the dough to knock out the air, then knead on a lightly floured work surface for 1 minute. Add the olives and knead until combined. Divide the dough in half, shape into 2 oval shapes 28 x 23 cm/11 x 9 inches long and place on the prepared baking sheets. Cover with oiled clingfilm and let stand in a warm place for 1 hour, or until the dough is puffy.

3 Press your fingers into the dough to make dimples, drizzle over 2 tablespoons of oil, and sprinkle with the rock salt. Bake in a preheated oven, 200°C/400°F/Gas Mark 6, for 30–35 minutes, or until golden. Drizzle with the remaining olive oil and cover with a cloth, to give a soft crust. Slice each loaf into 6 pieces and serve warm.

focaccia with roasted cherry tomatoes, basil & crispy pancetta

ingredients

SERVES 4–6

500 g/1 lb 2 oz white bread flour, plus extra for kneading and rolling

1 tbsp dried basil

1/2 tsp sugar

2 tsp rapid-rise dried yeast

2 tsp salt

325 ml/11 fl oz lukewarm water

2 tbsp olive oil, plus extra for oiling

topping

400 g/14 oz cherry tomatoes

1 tbsp olive oil, plus extra for oiling and drizzling

200 g/7 oz thick pancetta, diced

4 tbsp chopped fresh basil

salt and pepper

method

1 Place the flour, dried basil, sugar, yeast and salt in a bowl. Combine the water and oil and mix with the dry ingredients to form a soft dough, adding more water if the dough appears too dry. Turn out onto a lightly floured work surface and knead for 10 minutes, until smooth and elastic. Place in a lightly oiled bowl and cover with clingfilm. Let stand in a warm place for 1 hour, or until doubled in size.

2 Place the tomatoes on a baking sheet covered with baking paper, sprinkle with oil and season to taste with salt and pepper. Bake in a preheated oven, 140°C/275°F/Gas Mark 1, for 30 minutes, until soft.

3 Increase the oven temperature to 220°C/425°F/Gas Mark 7. Remove the dough from the bowl and knead again briefly. Shape into a rectangle and place on a lightly oiled baking sheet, turning the dough over to oil both sides. Make rough indentations in the dough using your fingers. Top with the tomatoes and pancetta. Sprinkle with salt and pepper. Let stand in a warm place for 10 minutes for the dough to rise again. Bake for 15–20 minutes, until golden and cooked through. Drizzle with oil and top with fresh basil. Serve warm.

mixed seed bread

ingredients

MAKES 1 MEDIUM LOAF

375 g/13 oz white bread flour,
plus extra for dusting

125 g/4^1/$_2$ oz rye flour

1^1/$_2$ tbsp skimmed milk
powder

1^1/$_2$ tsp salt

1 tbsp brown sugar

1 tsp easy-blend dried yeast

1^1/$_2$ tbsp sunflower oil

2 tsp lemon juice

300 ml/10 fl oz lukewarm
water

1 tsp caraway seeds

^{1}/$_2$ tsp poppy seeds

^{1}/$_2$ tsp sesame seeds

vegetable oil, for brushing

topping

1 egg white

1 tbsp water

1 tbsp sunflower or
pumpkin seeds

method

1 Place the flours, milk powder, salt, sugar and yeast in a large bowl. Pour in the oil and add the lemon juice and water. Stir in the seeds and mix well to make a smooth dough.

2 Turn the dough out onto a lightly floured work surface and knead for 10 minutes, or until the dough is smooth and elastic. Place the dough in an oiled bowl, cover with clingfilm and let stand in a warm place to rise for 1 hour, or until it has doubled in size.

3 Oil a 900-g/2-lb loaf tin. Turn the dough out onto a lightly floured work surface and knead for 1 minute until smooth. Shape the dough the length of the tin and three times the width. Fold the dough into three lengthways and place it in the tin with the join underneath. Cover and let stand in a warm place for 30 minutes until it has risen above the tin.

4 For the topping, lightly beat the egg white with the water to make a glaze. Just before baking, brush the glaze over the loaf, then gently press the sunflower or pumpkin seeds all over the top.

5 Bake in a preheated oven, 220°C/425°F/ Gas Mark 7, for 30 minutes, or until firm and golden brown. Test that the loaf is cooked by tapping it on the bottom – it should sound hollow. Transfer to a wire rack to cool completely before serving.

cheese & chive plait

ingredients

SERVES 10

450 g/1 lb strong white bread flour, plus extra for dusting

1 tsp salt

1 tsp caster sugar

1$\frac{1}{2}$ tsp easy-blend dried yeast

2 tbsp butter

115 g/4 oz coarsely grated Cheddar cheese

3 tbsp snipped fresh chives

4 spring onions, chopped

150 ml/5 fl oz tepid milk

175 ml/6 fl oz tepid water

vegetable oil, for brushing

beaten egg, for glazing

method

1 Sift the flour and salt into a warmed bowl and stir in the sugar and yeast. Rub in the butter, then stir in the cheese, chives and spring onions. Make a well in the centre. Mix together the milk and water, pour into the well and mix to make a soft dough. Turn the dough out onto a lightly floured work surface and knead for 10 minutes, or until smooth and elastic.

2 Transfer the dough to a clean, oiled bowl and cover with clingfilm. Let stand in a warm place for 1 hour, or until doubled in size. Brush a large baking sheet with oil. Turn the dough out onto a floured work surface and knead for 1 minute. Divide the dough into 3 pieces. Roll out each piece into a rope shape and plait the 3 pieces together, pinching the ends to seal.

3 Place on the prepared baking sheet and cover with oiled clingfilm. Let stand in a warm place for 45 minutes, or until doubled in size. Brush with beaten egg and bake in a preheated oven, 220°C/425°F/Gas Mark 7, for 20 minutes.

4 Reduce the oven temperature to 180°C/ 350°F/Gas Mark 4 and bake for a further 15 minutes, or until golden brown and the loaf sounds hollow when tapped on the bottom. Serve warm or cold.

english muffins

ingredients

MAKES 10–12

2 x 7-g/^{1}/$_4$-oz sachets
    easy-blend dried yeast
250 ml/9 fl oz tepid water
125 ml/4 fl oz natural yogurt
450 g/1 lb strong plain flour
^{1}/$_2$ tsp salt
50 g/1^3/$_4$ oz fine semolina
vegetable oil, for greasing
butter and jam (optional),
    to serve

method

1 Mix the yeast with half the tepid water in a bowl until it has dissolved. Add the remaining water and the yogurt and mix well.

2 Sift the flour into a large bowl and add the salt. Pour in the yeast liquid and mix well to a soft dough. Turn out onto a floured work surface and knead well until very smooth. Put the dough back into the bowl, cover with clingfilm and let rise for 30–40 minutes in a warm place until it has doubled in size.

3 Turn out again onto the work surface and knead lightly. Roll out the dough to a thickness of 2 cm/¾ inch. Using a 7.5-cm/ 3-inch cutter, cut into rounds and scatter the semolina over each muffin. Re-roll the trimmings of the dough and make further muffins until it is all used up. Place them on a lightly floured baking sheet, cover and let rise again for 30–40 minutes.

4 Heat a large frying pan and lightly grease with a a piece of scrunched-up kitchen paper dipped in vegetable oil. Cook half the muffins for 7–8 minutes on each side, taking care not to burn them. Repeat with the rest of the muffins. Serve at once with lots of butter and jam, if liked.

cheese & tomato pizza

ingredients

SERVES 2

dough

225 g/8 oz plain flour, plus
  extra for dusting

1 tsp salt

1 tsp easy-blend dried yeast

1 tbsp olive oil, plus extra
  for brushing

6 tbsp lukewarm water

topping

6 tomatoes, sliced thinly

175 g/6 oz mozzarella
  cheese, drained and
  sliced thinly

2 tbsp shredded fresh basil
  leaves

2 tbsp olive oil

salt and pepper

method

1 To make the pizza dough, sift the flour and salt into a bowl and stir in the yeast. Make a well in the centre and pour in the oil and water. Gradually incorporate the dry ingredients into the liquid, using a wooden spoon or floured hands.

2 Turn out the dough onto a lightly floured work surface and knead well for 5 minutes, until smooth and elastic. Return to the clean bowl, cover with lightly oiled clingfilm and set aside to rise in a warm place for about 1 hour, or until doubled in size.

3 Turn out the dough onto a lightly floured work surface and knock down. Knead briefly, then cut it in half and roll out each piece into a circle about 5 mm/¼ inch thick. Transfer to a lightly oiled baking sheet and push up the edges with your fingers to form a small rim.

4 For the topping, arrange the tomato and mozzarella slices alternately over the pizza bases. Season to taste with salt and pepper, sprinkle with the basil and drizzle with the olive oil. Bake in a preheated oven, 230°C/450°F/Gas Mark 8, for 15–20 minutes, until the crust is crisp and the cheese has melted. Serve immediately.

blinis

ingredients

MAKES 8

115 g/4 oz buckwheat flour
115 g/4 oz white bread flour
7-g/¹/₄-oz sachet easy-blend
    dried yeast
1 tsp salt
375 ml/13 fl oz tepid milk
2 eggs, 1 whole and
    1 separated
vegetable oil, for brushing
soured cream and smoked
    salmon, to serve

method

1 Sift both flours into a large, warmed bowl. Stir in the yeast and salt. Beat in the milk, whole egg and egg yolk until smooth. Cover the bowl and let stand in a warm place for 1 hour.

2 Place the egg white in a spotlessly clean bowl and whisk until soft peaks form. Fold into the batter. Brush a heavy-based frying pan with oil and set over medium–high heat. When the frying pan is hot, pour enough of the batter onto the surface to make a blini about the size of a saucer.

3 When bubbles rise, turn the blini over with a spatula and cook the other side until light brown. Wrap in a clean tea towel to keep warm while cooking the remainder. Serve the warm blinis with soured cream and smoked salmon.

savoury nibbles

This chapter has recipes for some really creative and exciting savoury tarts and tartlets, which will please your family and wow your guests at a lunch or supper party; savoury muffins, great for lunchboxes or taking on picnics; and crisp little bites to serve as appetizers with drinks.

Making pastry can be a chore if time is short, so you can use ready-made pastry for the savoury tarts if this is more convenient. However, the Spring Vegetable Tart and the Yellow Courgette Tart have a little Parmesan cheese in the pastry and this really adds a special touch, so try to make this if you can. Tartlets are especially good for serving at a buffet – they are all delicious, and Artichoke & Pancetta, Smoked Salmon, Dill & Horseradish and Feta & Spinach are particularly stylish.

You can pack a lot of goodness into a muffin, so they are great for snacks – Leek & Ham Muffins, Herb Muffins with Smoked Cheese and Soured Cream Muffins with Chives will appeal to younger children, and the others to those with a more sophisticated taste!

Home-baked savoury nibbles are so impressive – serve Spiced Cocktail Bites, Pesto Palmiers or Cheese & Rosemary Sables to get a dinner party off to an excellent start!

triple tomato tart

ingredients

SERVES 6

250 g/9 oz ready-made puff
  pastry

topping

3 tbsp sundried tomato paste

250 g/9 oz ripe vine tomatoes,
  sliced

150 g/5$^{1}/_{2}$ oz cherry tomatoes,
  cut in half

2 sprigs fresh rosemary

2 tbsp extra-virgin olive oil

1 tbsp balsamic vinegar

1 egg yolk

125 g/4$^{1}/_{2}$ oz Italian sliced
  salami, chopped

salt and pepper

handful of thyme sprigs

method

1 Roll out the dough to form a rectangle 35 cm/14 inches long and 25 cm/10 inches wide and lift onto a heavy-duty baking sheet. Spread the sundried tomato paste over the dough, leaving a 3-cm/1$^{1}/_{4}$-inch margin round the edge. Arrange the vine tomato slices over the tomato paste, sprinkle over the cherry tomato halves and top with the rosemary. Drizzle with 1 tablespoon of the olive oil and the balsamic vinegar.

2 Brush the edges of the dough with the egg yolk and bake in a preheated oven, 190°C/375°F/Gas Mark 5, for 10 minutes. Sprinkle over the chopped salami and bake for a further 10–15 minutes.

3 Remove the tart from the oven and season to taste with salt and pepper. Drizzle with the remaining olive oil and sprinkle with the thyme.

crab & watercress tart

ingredients

SERVES 6

pastry

125 g/4¹/2 oz plain flour

pinch of salt

75 g/2¹/2 oz cold butter,
   cut into pieces, plus extra
   for greasing

cold water

filling

300 g/10¹/2 oz prepared white
   and brown crabmeat

1 bunch watercress, washed
   and leaves picked from
   stems

50 ml/2 fl oz milk

2 large eggs, plus 3 egg yolks

200 ml/7 fl oz double cream

¹/2 tsp ground nutmeg

¹/2 bunch fresh chives, snipped

2 tbsp finely grated Parmesan
   cheese

salt and pepper

fresh sprigs of watercress,
   to garnish

method

1 Lightly grease a 23-cm/9-inch loose-based fluted tart tin. Sift the flour and salt into a food processor, add the butter and process until the mixture resembles fine breadcrumbs. Add just enough cold water to bring the dough together.

2 Turn out onto a floured work surface and roll out the dough 8 cm/3¹/4 inches larger than the tin. Carefully lift the dough into the tin and press to fit. Roll the rolling pin over the tin to neaten the edges and trim the excess dough. Fit a piece of baking paper into the tart case, fill with dried beans and chill in the refrigerator for 30 minutes.

3 Remove the pastry case from the refrigerator and bake blind for 10 minutes in a preheated oven, 190°C/375°F/Gas Mark 5, then remove the beans and paper. Return to the oven for 5 minutes. Remove the tin from the oven and lower the oven temperature to 160°C/325°F/Gas Mark 3.

4 Arrange the crabmeat and watercress in the tart tin. Whisk the milk, eggs and egg yolks together in a bowl. Bring the cream to simmering point in a pan and pour over the egg mixture, whisking all the time. Season with salt, pepper and nutmeg and stir in the chives. Carefully pour this mixture over the crab and watercress and sprinkle over the Parmesan. Bake for 35–40 minutes, until golden and set. Let the tart stand for 10 minutes before serving with sprigs of watercress.

goat's cheese & thyme tart

ingredients

SERVES 6

250 g/9 oz ready-made puff
    pastry

topping

500 g/1 lb 2 oz goat's cheese,
    such as chèvre, sliced
3–4 sprigs fresh thyme,
    leaves picked from stalks
55 g/2 oz black olives, pitted
50 g/1¾ oz tinned anchovies
    in olive oil
1 tbsp olive oil
1 egg yolk
salt and pepper
sprigs of fresh thyme, to
    garnish

method

1 Roll the dough into a large circle or rectangle and place on a baking sheet.

2 Arrange the cheese slices on the dough, leaving a 2.5-cm/1-inch margin round the edge. Sprinkle the thyme and olives, then arrange the anchovies, over the cheese. Drizzle over the olive oil. Season well with salt and pepper and brush the edges of the dough with the egg yolk.

3 Bake in a preheated oven, 190°C/375°F/Gas Mark 5, for 20–25 minutes, until the cheese is bubbling and the pastry is browned. Garnish with sprigs of fresh thyme.

spring vegetable tart

ingredients

pastry

250 g/9 oz plain flour

pinch of salt

125 g/4$^{1}/_{2}$ oz cold butter,
    cut into pieces

55 g/2 oz grated Parmesan
    cheese

1 egg

1 tbsp cold water

filling

300 g/11 oz selection of baby
    spring vegetables, such
    as carrots, asparagus,
    peas, broad beans, spring
    onions, corn cobs and
    leeks, trimmed and peeled
    where necessary

300 ml/10 fl oz double cream

125 g/4$^{1}/_{2}$ oz mature Cheddar
    cheese, grated

2 eggs plus 3 egg yolks

handful of fresh tarragon and
    flatleaf parsley, chopped

salt and pepper

method

1 Grease a 25-cm/10-inch loose-based tart tin. Sift the flour and salt into a food processor, add the butter and pulse to combine, then tip into a large bowl and add the Parmesan cheese. Mix the egg and water together in a small bowl. Add most of the egg mixture and work into a soft dough, using more egg mixture if needed. Turn out onto a floured work surface and roll out the dough 8 cm/3$^{1}/_{4}$ inches larger than the tin. Carefully lift the dough into the tin and press to fit. Roll the rolling pin over the tin to trim the excess dough. Fit a piece of baking paper into the tart case, fill with dried beans and chill in the refrigerator for 30 minutes.

2 Bake the tart case blind for 15 minutes in a preheated oven, 200°C/400°F/Gas Mark 6, then remove the beans and paper and bake for a further 5 minutes. Remove from the oven and cool. Lower the oven temperature to 180°C/350°F/Gas Mark 4.

3 Cut the vegetables into bite-sized pieces and blanch in boiling water. Drain and cool. Bring the cream to simmering point in a pan. Place the cheese, eggs and egg yolks in a heatproof bowl and pour the warm cream over the mixture. Stir to combine, season well and stir in the herbs. Arrange the vegetables in the tart case, pour over the cheese filling and bake for 30–40 minutes, until set. Cool in the tin for 10 minutes before serving.

yellow courgette tart

ingredients

SERVES 6

1 quantity cheese pastry
  (see page 178)

filling

2 large yellow courgettes

1 tbsp salt

3 heaped tbsp unsalted butter

1 bunch spring onions,
  trimmed and finely sliced

150 ml/5 fl oz double cream

3 large eggs

1 small bunch of fresh chives,
  chopped

salt and white pepper

method

1 Grease a 25-cm/10-inch loose-based tart tin. Roll out the pastry 8 cm/3^{1}/$_{4}$ inches larger than the tin. Carefully lift the dough into the tin and press to fit. Roll the rolling pin over the tin to neaten the edges and trim the excess dough. Fit a piece of baking paper into the tart case, fill with dried beans and chill in the refrigerator for 30 minutes.

2 Bake the tart case blind for 15 minutes in a preheated oven, 200°C/400°F/Gas Mark 6, then remove the beans and paper and bake for a further 5 minutes. Remove from the oven and cool. Lower the oven temperature to 180°C/350°F/Gas Mark 4.

3 Meanwhile, grate the courgettes and put in a sieve with 1 tablespoon of salt. Drain for 20 minutes, then rinse and put in a clean tea towel, squeezing all the moisture from the courgettes. Keep dry.

4 Melt the butter in a wide frying pan, sauté the spring onions until soft, then add the courgettes and cook over medium heat for 5 minutes, until any liquid has evaporated. Cool slightly. Whisk the cream and eggs together with the salt and pepper and chives. Spoon the courgettes into the tart case and pour in the cream mixture, making sure it settles properly, then bake for 30 minutes. Serve the tart hot or cold.

squash, sage & gorgonzola tart

ingredients

SERVES 6

1 quantity pastry
  (see page 174)

filling

1/2 small butternut squash or
  1 slice pumpkin, weighing
  250 g/9 oz
1 tsp olive oil
250 ml/9 fl oz double cream
175 g/6 oz Gorgonzola cheese
2 eggs, plus 1 egg yolk
6–8 fresh sage leaves
salt and pepper

method

1 Cut the squash in half and brush the cut side with the oil. Place cut-side up on a baking sheet and bake for 30–40 minutes, until browned and very soft. Set aside to cool. Remove the seeds and scoop out the flesh into a large bowl, discarding the skin.

2 Lightly grease a 23-cm/9-inch loose-based fluted tart tin. Roll out the pastry 8 cm/ 3 1/4 inches larger than the tin. Lift the dough into the tin and press to fit. Roll the rolling pin over the tin to trim the excess dough. Fit a piece of baking paper into the tart case and fill it with dried beans. Chill in the refrigerator for 30 minutes, then bake blind for 10 minutes in a preheated oven, 190°C/375°F/Gas Mark 5. Remove the beans and paper and return to the oven for 5 minutes.

3 Mash the squash and mix it with half the cream, season with salt and pepper, then spread it in the pastry case. Slice the cheese and lay it on top. Whisk the remaining cream with the eggs and egg yolk and pour the mixture into the tart tin, making sure it settles evenly. Arrange the sage leaves in a circle on the surface. Bake for 30–35 minutes and leave for 10 minutes in the tin before serving.

artichoke & pancetta tartlets

ingredients

MAKES 6 TARTLETS

1 quantity pastry
(see page 174)

filling

5 tbsp double cream
4 tbsp bottled artichoke paste
400 g/14 oz canned artichoke
hearts, drained
12 thin-cut pancetta slices
rocket leaves
50 g/1¾ oz Parmesan or
pecorino cheese
2 tbsp olive oil, for drizzling
salt and pepper

method

1 Grease 6 x 9-cm/3½-inch loose-based fluted tart tins. Divide the pastry into 6 pieces. Roll each piece to fit the tart tins. Carefully fit each piece of dough in its tin and press well to fit. Roll the rolling pin over the tin to trim the excess dough. Cut 6 pieces of baking paper and fit a piece into each tart, fill with dried beans and chill in the refrigerator for 30 minutes.

2 Bake the tart cases for 10 minutes in a preheated oven, 200°C/400°F/Gas Mark 6, and then remove the beans and baking paper.

3 Meanwhile, stir the cream and the artichoke paste together and season well with salt and pepper. Divide between the pastry cases, spreading out to cover the base of each tart. Cut each artichoke heart into 3 pieces and divide between the tarts, curl 2 slices of the pancetta into each tart and bake for 10 minutes.

4 To serve, top each tart with a good amount of rocket then, using a potato peeler, sprinkle shavings of the Parmesan cheese over the tarts, drizzle with olive oil and serve at once.

smoked salmon, dill & horseradish tartlets

ingredients

MAKES 6 TARTLETS

1 quantity pastry
(see page 174)

filling

125 ml/4 fl oz soured cream
1 tsp creamed horseradish
$1/2$ tsp lemon juice
1 tsp Spanish capers,
chopped
3 egg yolks
200 g/7 oz smoked salmon
trimmings
bunch fresh dill, chopped
salt and pepper

method

1 Grease 6 x 9-cm/3$1/2$-inch loose-based fluted tart tins. Divide the pastry into 6 pieces. Roll each piece to fit the tart tins. Carefully fit each piece of dough in its tin and press well to fit. Roll the rolling pin over the tin to trim the excess dough. Cut 6 pieces of baking paper and fit a piece into each tart, fill with dried beans and chill in the refrigerator for 30 minutes.

2 Bake the tart cases for 10 minutes in a preheated oven, 200°C/400°F/Gas Mark 6, and then remove the beans and baking paper.

3 Meanwhile, put the soured cream, horseradish, lemon juice, capers and salt and pepper into a bowl and mix well. Add the egg yolks, the smoked salmon and the dill and carefully mix again. Divide this mixture between the tart cases and return to the oven for 10 minutes. Cool in the tins for 5 minutes before serving.

feta & spinach tartlets

ingredients

MAKES 6 TARTLETS

1 quantity pastry
   (see page 174) with
   $1/2$ nutmeg, freshly grated,
   added to the flour

filling

225 g/8 oz baby spinach
2 tbsp butter
150 ml/5 fl oz double cream
3 egg yolks
125 g/4$1/2$ oz feta cheese
25 g/1 oz pine nuts
salt and pepper
cherry tomatoes and sprigs of
   flat-leaf parsley, to garnish

method

1 Grease 6 x 9-cm/3$1/2$-inch loose-based fluted tart tins. Divide the pastry into 6 pieces. Roll each piece to fit the tart tins. Carefully fit each piece of dough in its tin and press well to fit. Roll the rolling pin over the tin to trim the excess dough. Cut 6 pieces of baking paper and fit a piece into each tart, then fill with dried beans and chill in the refrigerator for 30 minutes.

2 Bake the tart cases for 10 minutes in a preheated oven, 200°C/400°F/Gas Mark 6, and then remove the beans and baking paper.

3 Blanch the spinach in boiling water for just 1 minute, then drain and press to squeeze all the water out. Chop the spinach. Melt the butter in a frying pan, add the spinach and cook gently to evaporate any remaining liquid. Season well with salt and pepper. Stir in the cream and egg yolks. Crumble the feta and divide between the tarts, top with the creamed spinach and bake for 10 minutes. Sprinkle the pine nuts over the tartlets and cook for a further 5 minutes. Garnish with cherry tomatoes and sprigs of flat-leaf parsley.

savoury leek
& ham muffins

ingredients

MAKES 12

2 tbsp sunflower or peanut
  oil, plus extra for oiling
  (if using)
1 leek, washed, trimmed
  and finely chopped
280 g/10 oz plain flour
2 tsp baking powder
$1/2$ tsp baking soda
1 large egg, lightly beaten
300 ml/10 fl oz thick strained
  plain yogurt
4 tbsp butter, melted
25 g/1 oz Cheddar cheese,
  grated
25 g/1 oz fresh chives,
  finely snipped
150 g/5$1/2$ oz cooked ham,
  chopped

method

1 Oil a 12-cup muffin tin with sunflower oil, or line it with 12 muffin paper liners. Heat the remaining oil in a frying pan, add the chopped leek and cook, stirring, over low heat for 2 minutes. Remove from the heat and cool.

2 Sift the flour, baking powder and baking soda into a large mixing bowl. In a separate bowl, lightly mix the egg, yogurt and melted butter together. Add the Cheddar cheese, chives, cooked leek and half of the chopped ham, then mix together well. Add the cheese mixture to the flour mixture, then gently stir together until just combined. Do not overstir the batter – it is fine for it to be a little lumpy.

3 Divide the muffin batter evenly between the 12 cups in the muffin tin or the paper liners (they should be about two-thirds full). Sprinkle over the remaining chopped ham, then transfer to a preheated oven, 200°C/400°F/Gas Mark 6. Bake for 20 minutes, or until risen and golden. Remove the muffins from the oven and serve warm, or place them on a wire rack to cool.

potato & pancetta muffins

ingredients

MAKES 12

1 tbsp sunflower or peanut
oil, plus extra for oiling
(if using)

3 shallots, finely chopped

350 g/12 oz self-raising flour

1 tsp salt

450 g/1 lb potatoes, cooked
and mashed

2 large eggs

350 ml/12 fl oz milk

125 ml/4 fl oz soured cream

1 tbsp finely snipped
fresh chives

150 g/5^1/$_2$ oz pancetta, grilled
and crumbled into pieces

4 tbsp grated Cheddar cheese

method

1 Oil a 12-cup muffin tin with sunflower oil,
or line it with 12 muffin paper liners. Heat the
remaining oil in a frying pan, add the chopped
shallots and cook, stirring, over low heat for
2 minutes. Remove from the heat and cool.

2 Sift the flour and salt into a large mixing
bowl. In a separate bowl, mix together the
mashed potatoes, eggs, milk, soured cream,
chives and half of the pancetta. Add the
potato mixture to the flour mixture and
then gently stir together until just combined.
Do not overstir the batter – it is fine for it to
be a little lumpy.

3 Divide the muffin batter evenly between the
12 cups in the muffin tin or the paper liners
(they should be about two-thirds full). Sprinkle
over the remaining pancetta, then sprinkle
over the grated Cheddar cheese. Transfer to a
preheated oven, 200°C/400°F/Gas Mark 6, and
bake for 20 minutes, or until risen and golden.
Remove the muffins from the oven and serve
warm, or place them on a wire rack to cool.

herb muffins with smoked cheese

ingredients

MAKES 12

1 tbsp sunflower or peanut
   oil, for oiling (if using)
280 g/10 oz plain flour
2 tsp baking powder
$1/2$ tsp baking soda
25 g/1 oz smoked hard
   cheese, grated
50 g/1$3/4$ oz fresh parsley,
   finely chopped
1 large egg, lightly beaten
300 ml/10 fl oz thick strained
   plain yogurt
4 tbsp butter, melted

method

1 Oil a 12-cup muffin tin with sunflower oil, or line it with 12 muffin paper liners. Sift the flour, baking powder and baking soda into a large mixing bowl. Add the smoked cheese and the parsley and mix together well.

2 In a separate bowl, lightly mix the egg, yogurt and melted butter together. Add the yogurt mixture to the flour mixture and then gently stir together until just combined. Do not overstir the batter – it is fine for it to be a little lumpy.

3 Divide the muffin batter evenly between the 12 cups in the muffin tin or the paper liners (they should be about two-thirds full), then transfer to a preheated oven, 200°C/400°F/ Gas Mark 6. Bake for 20 minutes, or until risen and golden. Remove the muffins from the oven and serve warm, or place them on a wire rack to cool.

soured cream muffins with chives

ingredients

MAKES 12

1 tbsp sunflower or peanut oil, for oiling (if using)

280 g/10 oz plain flour

2 tsp baking powder

$1/2$ tsp baking soda

25 g/1 oz Cheddar cheese, grated

35 g/$1^1/4$ oz fresh chives, finely snipped, plus extra to garnish

1 large egg, lightly beaten

200 ml/7 fl oz soured cream

100 ml/$3^1/2$ fl oz plain unsweetened yogurt

4 tbsp butter, melted

method

1 Oil a 12-cup muffin tin with sunflower oil, or line it with 12 muffin paper liners. Sift the flour, baking powder and baking soda into a large mixing bowl. Add the cheese and chives and mix together well.

2 In a separate bowl, lightly mix the egg, soured cream, yogurt and melted butter together. Add the soured cream mixture to the flour mixture and then gently stir together until just combined. Do not overstir the batter – it is fine for it to be a little lumpy.

3 Divide the muffin batter evenly between the 12 cups in the muffin tin or the paper liners (they should be about two-thirds full). Sprinkle over the remaining snipped chives to garnish and transfer to a preheated oven, 200°C/400°F/Gas Mark 6. Bake for 20 minutes, or until risen and golden. Remove the muffins from the oven and serve warm, or place them on a wire rack to cool.

spiced cocktail bites

ingredients

MAKES ABOUT 20

115 g/4 oz butter, plus extra
  for greasing

140 g/5 oz plain flour, plus
  extra for dusting

2 tsp curry powder

85 g/3 oz grated Cheddar
  cheese

2 tsp poppy seeds

1 tsp black onion seeds

1 egg yolk

cumin seeds, for sprinkling

method

1 Grease 2 baking sheets with a little butter. Sift the flour and curry powder into a bowl. Cut the butter into pieces and add to the flour. Rub in until the mixture resembles breadcrumbs, then stir in the cheese, poppy seeds and black onion seeds. Stir in the egg yolk and mix to a firm dough.

2 Wrap the dough in clingfilm and chill in the refrigerator for 30 minutes. On a floured work surface, roll out the dough to 3 mm/^{1}/8 inch thick. Stamp out shapes with a cutter. Re-roll the trimmings and stamp out more shapes until the dough is used up.

3 Place the biscuits on the prepared baking sheets and sprinkle with the cumin seeds. Chill for a further 15 minutes. Bake in a preheated oven, 190°C/375°F/Gas Mark 5, for 20 minutes, or until crisp and golden. Serve warm or transfer to wire racks to cool.

savoury curried bites

ingredients

MAKES 40

100 g/3^1/$_2$ oz butter, softened,
   plus extra for greasing
100 g/3^1/$_2$ oz plain flour,
   plus extra for dusting
1 tsp salt
2 tsp curry powder
100 g/3^1/$_2$ oz grated mature
   Cheddar cheese
100 g/3^1/$_2$ oz freshly grated
   Parmesan cheese

method

1 Lightly grease about 4 baking sheets with a little butter.

2 Sift the flour and salt into a mixing bowl. Stir in the curry powder and both the grated cheeses. Rub in the softened butter with your fingertips, then bring the mixture together to form a soft dough.

3 Roll out the dough thinly on a lightly floured work surface to form a rectangle. Cut out 40 circles using a 5-cm/2-inch biscuit cutter and arrange on the baking sheets. Bake in a preheated oven, 180°C/350°F/Gas Mark 4, for 10–15 minutes, until golden brown.

4 Let the biscuits cool slightly on the baking sheets, then transfer them to a wire rack to cool completely and crispen.

pesto palmiers

ingredients

MAKES 20

butter, for greasing

plain flour, for dusting

250 g/9 oz ready-made
    puff pastry

3 tbsp green or red pesto

1 egg yolk, beaten with
    1 tbsp water

25 g/1 oz freshly grated
    Parmesan cheese

sprigs of fresh basil, to
    garnish

method

1 Grease a baking sheet with a little butter. On a floured work surface, roll out the pastry to a 35 x 15-cm/14 x 6-inch rectangle and trim the edges with a sharp knife. Spread the pesto evenly over the pastry. Roll up the ends tightly to meet in the centre of the pastry.

2 Wrap in clingfilm and chill in the refrigerator for 20 minutes, until firm, then remove from the refrigerator and unwrap. Brush with the beaten egg yolk on all sides. Cut across into 1-cm/^{1}/$_{2}$-inch thick slices. Place the slices on the prepared baking sheet.

3 Bake in a preheated oven, 200°C/400°F/ Gas Mark 6, for 10 minutes, or until crisp and golden. Remove from the oven and immediately sprinkle over the Parmesan cheese. Serve the palmiers warm or transfer to a wire rack and cool to room temperature. Garnish with sprigs of fresh basil.

cheese straws

ingredients

MAKES 24

115 g/4 oz plain flour, plus
   extra for dusting
pinch of salt
1 tsp curry powder
55 g/2 oz butter, plus extra
   for greasing
55 g/2 oz grated Cheddar
   cheese
1 egg, beaten
poppy and cumin seeds,
   for sprinkling

method

1 Sift the flour, salt and curry powder into a bowl. Add the butter and rub in until the mixture resembles breadcrumbs. Add the cheese and half the egg and mix to form a dough. Wrap in clingfilm and chill in the refrigerator for 30 minutes.

2 Lightly grease several baking sheets. On a floured work surface, roll out the dough to 5-mm/$1/4$-inch thick. Cut into 7.5 x 1-cm/ 3 x $1/2$-inch strips. Pinch the strips lightly along the sides and place on the prepared baking sheets.

3 Brush the straws with the remaining egg and sprinkle half with poppy seeds and half with cumin seeds. Bake in a preheated oven, 200°C/400°F/Gas Mark 6, for 10–15 minutes, or until golden. Transfer to wire racks to cool.

cheese & rosemary sables

ingredients

MAKES 40

225 g/8 oz cold butter, diced,
  plus extra for greasing
250 g/9 oz plain flour
250 g/9 oz grated Gruyère
  cheese
$1/2$ tsp cayenne pepper
2 tsp finely chopped fresh
  rosemary leaves
1 egg yolk, beaten with
  1 tbsp water

method

1 Lightly grease 2 baking sheets. Place the flour, butter, cheese, cayenne pepper and chopped rosemary in a food processor. Pulse until the mixture forms a dough, adding a little cold water, if necessary, to bring the mixture together.

2 On a floured work surface, roll out the dough to 5 mm/$1/4$ inch thick. Stamp out shapes such as stars and hearts with 6-cm/$2^{1}/2$-inch biscuit cutters.

3 Place the shapes on the prepared baking sheets, then cover with clingfilm and chill in the refrigerator for 30 minutes, or until firm. Brush with the beaten egg yolk and bake in a preheated oven, 180°C/350°F/Gas Mark 4, for 10 minutes, or until golden brown. Cool on the baking sheets for 2 minutes, then serve warm or transfer to wire racks to cool.